THE COMPLETE
GUIDE *to*
GRACE

JAMES L. LEFLER

THE COMPLETE GUIDE to GRACE

JAMES L. LEFLER

Silverday Press
P. O. Box 1011
Downers Grove, Illinois 60515
www.SilverdayPress.com

The Complete Guide to Grace

Published by Silverday Press – www.SilverdayPress.com

Printed in the United States of America.

Library of Congress Control Number: 2008906457

ISBN 13: 978-0-9729903-3-2

Cover Design: Pam Hamilton
                www.pamhamdesign.com

Table of Contents

Introduction

My study of grace has radically changed how I view God. He is closer, more patient and more involved in my daily activities than I ever imagined. Understanding all the ways He shows his favor gave me a new perspective of the blessings and challenges of life.

The first half of *The Complete Guide to Grace* describes the principles of grace, mercy and forgiveness, and presents what Noah, Gideon, Moses, Abraham and Paul discovered about grace, faith and obedience. The last half is devoted to practical applications of these principles in our own lives.

I used two translations of the Bible throughout this book. Where the meaning of words in the original Hebrew and Greek texts is key to understanding a scripture, I used the New American Standard Bible because it is a more literal translation. Otherwise, I used the New International Version for its clarity and readability.

If you are using *The Complete Guide to Grace* in a small group study or Bible class, I invite you to visit www.SilverdayPress.com to download a class outline and other free materials. The questions at the end of each chapter will also help you apply what is presented.

My prayer is that your relationship with God will be strengthened as a result of your study and you will enjoy the fullest measure of His grace.

Jim Lefler

Chapter 1

Grace, Mercy & Forgiveness

What is the grace of God? We often hear explanations that do more to muddy the water than clarify the meaning. To explain God's grace, people often talk about mercy. Sometimes grace sounds more like forgiveness or salvation. Many times the words "grace," "mercy" and "forgiveness" are used interchangeably. So it is not surprising that many people are confused about the meaning of grace and the impact God's grace has on their lives.

The way we use the words "grace" and "mercy" in normal everyday conversation can add to the confusion. For example, we may say, "Give me a little grace," when we want someone who is upset with us to get over their hurt feelings and let us out of the doghouse. However, as we shall see in a moment, it would be more appropriate to say, "Give me a little mercy." Similarly, a father who decides not to discipline his son might explain his leniency by saying, "I gave him grace." But a more accurate statement would be, "I showed him mercy." The significance of this is that even the casual misuse of spiritually significant words can contribute to the problem of misunderstanding God's grace.

When I ask people to define grace, mercy and forgiveness, or explain how they are different, I get a variety of responses, including silence, which is often followed by a request that I answer my own question. That is the focus of this chapter. We will examine the meanings of the Greek words translated "grace," "mercy" and "forgiveness," then present simple descriptions of these spiritual principles that will help us in our study of God's grace.

Grace:

The Greek word translated as "grace" in the New American Standard Bible (NASB) New Testament is *charis*. Though "grace" is by far the most frequent translation (122 times), *charis* is also translated as these other English words (number of times in parenthesis): favor (11), blessing (1), concession (1), credit (3), gift (1), gracious (2), gracious work (3), gratitude (1), thank (3), thankfulness (2), thanks (6). Note that *charis* is never translated "mercy" or "forgiveness."

The NASB translators used twelve different English words to communicate the meaning of the Greek word *charis*. The definition of *charis* helps us understand why:

> **Definition of *charis*:** 1. a winning quality or attractiveness that invites a favorable reaction, *graciousness, attractiveness, charm, winsomeness*; 2. a beneficent disposition toward someone, *favor, grace, gracious care/help, goodwill*; 3. a practical application of goodwill, *(a sign of) favor, gracious deed/gift, benefaction*; 4. an exceptional effect produced by generosity, *favor;* 5. a response to generosity or beneficence, *thanks, gratitude.*[1]

Understanding grace (*charis*) does not have to be complicated. When the New Testament was written, *charis* was not a theological concept that was difficult to describe. Instead, the number of times and various ways *charis* was used shows that it was part of normal everyday conversation. Its usage and meaning was easily understood. That thought is reinforced by the following passages that illustrate the five aspects of the definition of *charis*.

---

1.   Walter Bauer, <u>A Greek-English Lexicon of the New Testament and Other Early Christian Literature</u>, 3rd ed., rev. and ed. Frederick W. Danker (Chicago: University of Chicago Press, 2000), pp.1079-1080. Hereafter cited as <u>BDAG</u>.

1. <u>A winning quality or attractiveness that invites a favorable reaction, *graciousness, attractiveness, charm, winsomeness.*</u>

> And all were speaking well of Him, and wondering at the gracious [*charis*] words which were falling from His lips; and they were saying, "Is this not Joseph's son?" [Emphasis added.]
>
> Luke 4:22 NASB

In this verse, *charis* is translated as "gracious." As Jesus began to teach in the synagogue in Nazareth, he spoke in a way that received a favorable response. We use the word "grace" to describe similar behavior today. People show grace when they stay calm and speak with kind and gentle words in a potentially upsetting situation. In Colossians 4:6, we are instructed that our conversation should always be full of grace.

2. <u>A beneficent disposition toward someone, *favor, grace, gracious care/help, goodwill.*</u>

> The angel said to her, "Do not be afraid, Mary; for you have found favor [*charis*] with God." [Emphasis added.]
>
> Luke 1:30 NASB

This verse gives us some insight into the practical nature of this quality of God. Here *charis* is translated as "favor." Mary had nothing to fear because God was watching over her life.

Charis was used in a similar way in the following two verses, which give us a glimpse into God's relationship with Jesus. In the first verse, *charis* is translated "grace" and in the second, it is translated "favor":

> The Child continued to grow and become strong, increasing in wisdom; and the grace [*charis*] of God was upon Him. [Emphasis added.]
>
> Luke 2:40 NASB

> And Jesus kept increasing in wisdom and stature, and in favor [*charis*] with God and men. [Emphasis added.]
>
> Luke 2:52 NASB

From the time Jesus was a baby, God's disposition toward him was one of grace and goodwill. And as Jesus got older, there was more and more evidence of God's favor in his life. This makes sense to us because Jesus is God's son, but in the following verse, we see that God also offers his favor to us.

> But God, being rich in mercy, because of His great love with which He loved us, even when we were dead in our transgressions, made us alive together with Christ (by <u>grace</u> [*charis*] you have been saved), and raised us up with Him, and seated us with Him in the heavenly places in Christ Jesus, so that in the ages to come He might show the surpassing riches of His <u>grace</u> [*charis*] in kindness toward us in Christ Jesus. For by <u>grace</u> [*charis*] you have been saved through faith; and that not of yourselves, it is the gift of God. [Emphasis added.]
>
> Ephesians 2:4-8 NASB

Three times in this passage *charis* is translated as "grace." It describes evidence of God's favorable disposition toward us.

3. <u>Practical application of goodwill, *(a sign of) favor, gracious deed/ gift, benefaction.*</u>

This aspect of the definition of *charis* reinforces the practical nature of *charis*. It is not just a quality of God, but man as well. We can be the benefactors of the favor and goodwill of God or other people, or be the ones showing favor and goodwill to others. The following verse is an example of the latter:

> But Festus, wishing to do the Jews a <u>favor</u> [*charis*], answered Paul and said, "Are you willing to go up to Jerusalem and stand trial before me on these charges?" [Emphasis added.]
>
> Acts 25:9 NASB

Charis describes what Festus did to express his goodwill and show favor to the Jews. Asking someone to do you a *charis* (favor) would be a similar use of the word.

The next passage describes how a group of concerned believers showed *charis* to Christians who lived in another city. Here *charis* is translated as "favor" and "gracious work."

> For I testify that according to their ability, and beyond their ability, *they gave* of their own accord, begging us with much urging for the <u>favor</u> [*charis*] of participation in the support of the saints, and *this,* not as we had expected, but they first gave themselves to the Lord and to us by the will of God. So we urged Titus that as he had previously made a beginning, so he would also complete in you this <u>gracious work</u> [*charis*] as well. [Emphasis added.]
>
> 2 Corinthians 8:3-6 NASB

The Macedonian churches gave generously to support the poor in Jerusalem, even though they hardly had enough for themselves. Their actions were seen as evidence of the grace of God.[2] The first use of *charis* was translated as "favor" to represent how they felt about being given the opportunity. (The NIV reads, "privilege of sharing.") The second use of *charis* was translated as "gracious work" to represent the action they took. (The NIV reads, "act of grace.")

In Paul's reference to a contribution collected in Corinth for the church in Jerusalem, the word *charis* was translated as "gift":

> When I arrive, whomever you may approve, I will send them with letters to carry your <u>gift</u> [*charis*] to Jerusalem. [Emphasis added.]
>
> 1 Corinthians 16:3 NASB

This "gift" was a practical application of the goodwill of the Corinthians toward Christians in Jerusalem. Here are two more verses that describe practical aspects of God's grace toward Christians:

> Then when he arrived and witnessed the <u>grace</u> [*charis*] of God, he rejoiced and *began* to encourage them all with resolute heart to remain *true* to the Lord. [Emphasis added.]
>
> Acts 11:23 NASB

---

2. 2 Corinthians 8:1-2

> And now I commend you to God and to the word of His <u>grace</u> [*charis*], which is able to build *you* up and to give *you* the inheritance among all those who are sanctified. [Emphasis added.]

> Acts 20:32 NASB

The grace of God changes things in our lives on a daily basis. That is why Paul was able to see evidence of the impact of God's grace. And because of God's grace (favor), we have His word to equip and strengthen us and help us be close to Him. Without it we would not even know it was possible.

4. <u>Exceptional effect produced by generosity, *favor.*</u>

The Macedonian churches were joyful and generous despite the fact that they were living in poverty.[3] They are an example of how the *charis* of God has an exceptional effect on those who receive it, and how it moves people to show it to others. That kind of response is described by the following verse:

> And God is able to make all grace [*charis*] abound to you, so that always having all sufficiency in everything, you may have an abundance for every good deed.

> 2 Corinthians 9:8 NASB

Throughout this book, we will see how God's grace changes lives. And the more we understand God's favor, the greater the impact it can have. The apostle Paul, for example, credited the grace of God for his complete transformation:

> But by the <u>grace</u> [*charis*] of God I am what I am, and His <u>grace</u> [*charis*] toward me did not prove vain; but I labored even more than all of them, yet not I, but the <u>grace</u> [*charis*] of God with me. [Emphasis added.]

> 1 Corinthians 15:10 NASB

Paul went from persecuting Christians to becoming a Christian, and building the church he once sought to destroy. The effect of God's grace goes far beyond what we might expect. By God's grace, what

---

3.   2 Corinthians 8:1-2

formerly seemed impossible becomes possible, and what once seemed illogical makes sense. Consider this example:

> And He has said to me, "My grace [*charis*] is sufficient for you, for power is perfected in weakness." Most gladly, therefore, I will rather boast about my weaknesses, so that the power of Christ may dwell in me.
>
> 2 Corinthians 12:9 NASB

With God's favor, even the weak become strong and powerful.

5. Response to generosity or beneficence; *thanks, gratitude.*

In the following passages, *charis* is translated as "thanks":

> But thanks [*charis*] be to God that though you were slaves of sin, you became obedient from the heart to that form of teaching to which you were committed. [Emphasis added.]
>
> Romans 6:17 NASB

> Thanks [*charis*] be to God for His indescribable gift! [Emphasis added.]
>
> 2 Corinthians 9:15 NASB

When you give someone a gift or say thank you for something you received, your actions can be described by the word *charis*. Saying thank you is a way to show favor in return for the favor you have received.

To summarize, if you could speak the Greek language, you might use *charis* to describe a special relationship you have with another person or even your relationship with God. *Charis* could represent the favor God feels toward you or a particular sign of that favor in your life. *Charis* could also represent a generous gift that you gave to someone as well as their thankful response.

In all of these applications, *charis* involves showing or receiving favor. So we can think of the *charis* of God as his favor. Many writers, in fact, have defined grace as God's favor, but they often add the adjective "unmerited" (unmerited favor). While is it true that God's favor is unearned, the idea of merit is not in the original text. This distinction may not seem important at first, but the impact can be significant.

It takes some thought to appreciate, but just mentioning merit as a consideration in any relationship can create doubts that are difficult to overcome. For example, if you thank a friend who did you a favor, he will likely say, "I was happy to do it." It is very unlikely he would say, "I did you an undeserved favor." If he did, you might ask, "Then why did you do it?" Bringing the issue of merit into the conversation could make you feel hurt or insecure, and do some damage to your relationship.

To illustrate further, if I were speaking to my two sons about how much I cared about them, I would never say, "You have my *unmerited* favor." If I did, I doubt it would encourage them at all. I love my sons because they are my sons. Merit has nothing to do with it. When I first held my newborn sons in my arms, whether they deserved my love or not never crossed my mind. Instead, I thought of all the things I wanted to do for them and the things I would teach them, and how I wanted to make them happy. It is natural for a father (and especially God) to love and show favor to his children.

God's interaction with Gideon will also help us see why bringing "unmerited" into the discussion of grace is not helpful. Gideon saw himself as the least in the weakest family in Manasseh,[4] but God sent his angel to convince Gideon that he was the one to lead the Israelites in battle against a powerful enemy. But if the angel of the Lord who called Gideon "mighty warrior" had said, "Oh, mighty, but undeserving warrior," it would have been more difficult than ever to convince Gideon that he had the favor of God. Merit had nothing to do with God showing favor to Gideon. In Chapter 3, we will see how God patiently helped Gideon realize that he had His favor.

To summarize, bringing merit into a discussion of God's grace can take our thoughts in the wrong direction. It can make us wonder if there is a limit to how much unmerited favor we will receive. If I do one more thing that disappoints God, will he decide that I have finally crossed the line and stop showing me favor? That is an insecure place to be.

---

4. Judges 6:15 NIV

When we focus on how undeserving we are to have God's favor, we end up thinking more about ourselves than about God. But God's favor has more to do with his loving nature than with how deserving or undeserving we are. So it would be better to focus on the nature of God and how he wants to show us his favor than to focus on our lack of merit.

We began this chapter with the question: What is the grace of God? The answer is simply the favor of God.

A Simple Description of God's Grace: The favor of God

Mercy:

In the NASB New Testament, the Greek word *eleos* is translated as "mercy" twenty-five times and twice as "compassion." *Eleos* is never translated as "grace" or "forgiveness," and *charis* is never translated as "mercy." Webster's Dictionary gives mercy as a synonym for grace,[5] but the biblical meanings of *eleos* and *charis* are very different.

Definition of *eleos*: Kindness or concern expressed for someone in need, *mercy, compassion, pity, clemency.*[6]

Eleeo, the verb form of *eleos*, is translated "have mercy" fifteen times in the NASB New Testament and these other words (number of times shown in parenthesis): had mercy (4), received mercy (3), shown mercy (3), has mercy (2), found mercy (1), receive mercy (1), show mercy (1), shows mercy (1), mercy (1).

Definition of *eleeo*: To be greatly concerned about someone in need, *have compassion/mercy/pity.* 1. exercise of benevolent goodwill, *alms, charitable giving*; 2. that which is benevolently given to meet a need, *alms.*[7]

---

5. Webster's New World College Dictionary, Fourth Edition (Cleveland, Ohio: Wiley Publishing, Inc., 2008), pp. 614-615.

6. BDAG, p.316.

7. BDAG, p.315.

The kindness or concern that we feel for someone might move us to forgive them, but *eleos* does not mean forgive. Rather, *eleos* is better thought of as an emotion we feel toward someone that moves us to want to offer them relief. *Eleos* is a quality that God has in abundance. God's kindness and concern for us was the reason he sent Jesus to die on the cross so we would not suffer eternally for our sins. His mercy (*eleos*) moved him to show favor (*charis*) by sending Jesus to offer us relief from our sins:

> But God, being rich in mercy [*eleos*], because of His great love with which He loved us, even when we were dead in our transgressions, made us alive together with Christ (by grace [*charis*] you have been saved).
>
> Ephesians 2:4-5 NASB

God was incredibly kind to us despite how unworthy we were. It would surely take great love and mercy to let your son die so the people who sinned against Him could live. Jesus demonstrated and taught about such mercy from the early days of his ministry. He even ate meals with tax collectors and people with a reputation for being sinners. When the Pharisees questioned why He did that, Jesus said, "Go and learn what this means: 'I desire compassion (*eleos*) and not sacrifice.'" This is one of only two places in the NASB where *eleos* is translated "compassion." (The NIV reads, "I desire mercy, not sacrifice.") Here is the full context of Jesus' remarks:

> Then it happened that as Jesus was reclining at the table in the house, behold, many tax collectors and sinners came and were dining with Jesus and His disciples. When the Pharisees saw this, they said to His disciples, "Why is your Teacher eating with the tax collectors and sinners?" But when Jesus heard this, He said, "It is not those who are healthy who need a physician, but those who are sick. But go and learn what this means: 'I desire compassion [*eleos*], and not sacrifice,' for I did not come to call the righteous, but sinners."
>
> Matthew 9:10-13 NASB

The Pharisees had no compassion (*eleos*) for tax collectors and sinners, and were indignant that Jesus did. In a similar fashion they responded without compassion when Jesus' disciples were so hungry they ate heads of grain they picked in the fields. The Pharisees reacted by charging that grain-picking was unlawful on the Sabbath. A compassionate response would have been to share their own food with Jesus' disciples so they would not have needed to eat raw grain. Jesus said, "If you had known what this means, 'I desire compassion (*eleos*), and not a sacrifice,' you would not have condemned the innocent."[8]

The Pharisees were willing to make many sacrifices, but they lacked compassion. In their hypocrisy, they were careful to tithe on the tiniest of their possessions (e.g., spices), but were not concerned about showing *eleos* (mercy/compassion).

> Woe to you, scribes and Pharisees, hypocrites! For you tithe mint and dill and cummin, and have neglected the weightier provisions of the law: justice and <u>mercy</u> [*eleos*] and faithfulness; but these are the things you should have done without neglecting the others. [Emphasis added.]
>
> Matthew 23:23 NASB

The story of the Good Samaritan in Luke 10:25-37 teaches us something else about *eleos*. To set the stage, a religious man has just recited the greatest commandment from memory. Jesus responded, "Do this and you will live." Then Jesus told the man about a priest and a Levite who came upon a fellow Jew who lay injured beside the road, but did nothing to help him. However, a Samaritan who came along did everything he could to help. "Which of these three do you think proved to be a neighbor to the man?" asked Jesus. The religious man replied, "The one who showed mercy [*eleos*]."[9]

We don't know what the priest and the Levite were thinking. Perhaps, "I'm too busy" or "I have more important things to do." Maybe they suspected that the man somehow brought this misery on himself.

---

8. Matthew 12:7 NASB

9. Luke 10:36-37 NASB

Regardless, they did not show compassion or offer the man any relief. We also do not know if the Samaritan knew anything at all about the injured man, but it did not seem to matter why the man happened to be on the road or how he got injured. The presence or absence of sin in the man's life apparently did not matter either, and, remarkably, it did not matter that Jews typically would not have associated with Samaritans. Despite all the potential reasons for not helping the man, the Samaritan did more than was expected. He even paid for a room in the inn where the man could rest and recover from his wounds. We can only imagine how grateful the injured man felt for the compassion shown him by the Samaritan.

Jesus told the religious man to go and do likewise. That direction applies to us as well. If we think we are too busy doing spiritual things to show compassion, we are too focused on sacrifice. And if we find reasons to justify not showing mercy, we have forgotten that Jesus did not come to call the righteous, but sinners.[10] Jesus had compassion on those who were suffering, even those who were suffering as a result of their sin.

We too must learn what Jesus meant when he said, "I desire compassion and not sacrifice." From his example, we learn that we must be willing to give of ourselves to show *eleos* (mercy/compassion) to people who are suffering. God has incredible mercy for us, and he calls us to show mercy to others:

> For judgment *will be* merciless to one who has shown no mercy [*eleos*]; mercy [*eleos*] triumphs over judgment.
>
> James 2:13 NASB

In summary, mercy or compassion is an emotion we feel that moves us to do what we can to help others find relief from their troubles or suffering.

A Simple Description of Mercy:
The compassion to offer relief

---

10. Matthew 9:13

Forgiveness:

Of the three principles—grace, mercy and forgiveness—forgiveness is probably the easiest for us to explain. But knowing what forgiveness means is only the beginning of fully appreciating what God has done for us by forgiving us.

The Greek word translated as "forgiveness" in the NASB is *aphesis*. It is translated "forgiveness" fifteen times, and once as "release" and once more as "free," as in "set free from oppression." No other Greek word is translated "forgiveness" in the NASB New Testament.

> **Definition of *aphesis*:** 1. the act of freeing and liberating from something that confines, *release*; 2. the act of freeing from an obligation, guilt, or punishment, *pardon, cancellation.*[11]

In the following verse *aphesis* is translated both "release" and "free."

> He has sent me to proclaim <u>release</u> [*aphesis*] to the captives, and recovery of sight to the blind, to set <u>free</u> [*en aphesis*] those who are oppressed. [Emphasis added.]
>
> Luke 4:18b NASB

Jesus described the purpose of his ministry as preaching *aphesis*. After he rose from the dead, Jesus reminded his disciples that it was prophesied that he would die and be raised again so *aphesis* of sins could be preached:

> And He said to them, "Thus it is written, that the Christ would suffer and rise again from the dead the third day, and that repentance for <u>forgiveness</u> [*aphesis*] of sins would be proclaimed in His name to all the nations, beginning from Jerusalem." [Emphasis added.]
>
> Luke 24:46-47 NASB

Jesus went to the cross so that his present and future disciples could be freed from their sins. A short time later, on the day of Pentecost, Peter preached that very message. It happened in Jerusalem, just as Jesus said it would. When the people understood the significance of

---

11. <u>BDAG</u>, p.155.

what had happened, and realized the gravity of their sins, they asked, "What shall we do?" Peter told them how they could be set free from their sins:

> Repent, and each of you be baptized in the name of Jesus Christ for the *forgiveness* [*aphesis*] of your sins; and you will receive the gift of the Holy Spirit.
>
> Acts 2:38 NASB

If they repented and were baptized in the name of Jesus, whom they had crucified, they could be released from the obligation to pay for their sins. On that day, over three thousand people responded by being baptized.[12] The following verse explains God's motivation for offering to release us from our sins:

> In Him we have redemption through His blood, the <u>forgiveness</u> [*aphesis*] of our trespasses, according to the riches of His grace [*charis*]. [Emphasis added.]
>
> Ephesians 1:7 NASB

This verse explains the connection between grace and forgiveness in simple terms. Forgiveness is possible because of the grace of God. Because of His favor, God gave us the opportunity to be forgiven of our sins.

Aphesis, the word translated as "forgiveness," is from *aphiemi*, the word most often translated "forgive."

Definition of *aphiemi*: 1. to dismiss or release someone or something from a place or one's presence; 2. to release from legal or moral obligation or consequence, *cancel, remit, pardon;* 3. to move away, with implication of causing a separation, *leave, depart from;* 4. to have something continue or remain in a place, *leave standing/lying* (without concerning oneself further about it); 5. to convey a sense of distancing

---

12. Acts 2:41

through an allowable margin of freedom, leave it to someone to do something, *let, let go, allow, tolerate.*[13]

Aphiemi had a broader meaning than *aphesis.* In the NASB, *aphiemi* is translated into twenty-five English words (number of times in parenthesis): left (38), forgive (23), forgiven (23), let (9), leaving (8), leave (7), let alone (6), permit (6), allow (5), and 16 other words either one or two times. *Aphiemi* is never translated as "mercy" or "grace." The NASB Greek-Hebrew Dictionary defines *aphiemi* as "to send away, leave alone or permit."[14] Here are some familiar verses using *aphiemi*:

> Immediately they left [*aphiemi*] their nets and followed Him. [Emphasis added.]
>
> Matthew 4:20 NASB

> Leave [*aphiemi*] your offering there before the altar and go; first be reconciled to your brother, and then come and present your offering. [Emphasis added.]
>
> Matthew 5:24 NASB

> He touched her hand, and the fever left [*aphiemi*] her; and she got up and waited on Him. [Emphasis added.]
>
> Matthew 8:15 NASB

In the first two verses, *aphiemi* described what happens when you leave something where it is and move away. For example, the disciples "left" (*aphiemi*) their nets to follow Jesus. In the last verse, *aphiemi* described how a separation was created when Peter's mother-in-law stayed where she was and her fever "left" (*aphiemi*). These are good examples of common uses of *aphiemi*. Now consider examples where *aphiemi* is used to communicate how we can be released from the consequences of our sin:

> And forgive [*aphiemi*] us our debts, as we also have forgiven [*aphiemi*] our debtors.
>
> Matthew 6:12 NASB

---

13. BDAG, p.156

14. NASB Greek-Hebrew Dictionary, WORD*search* 8.0.2.40 (WORD*search* Corp, 2008).

> Blessed are those whose lawless deeds have been forgiven,
> [*aphiemi*] and whose sins have been covered.

Romans 4:7 NASB

Understanding the common uses of *aphiemi* paints a good mental picture of what *aphiemi* means with regard to our sin. We get to leave our sins behind! Remember that the word translated forgiveness (*aphesis*) is taken from *aphiemi* and describes the act of freeing and liberating someone from an obligation or punishment. We get to go forward and live a new life for God without the burden of our sins being dragged around like a ball and chain.

Getting to leave our sins behind is a good description of what it means to be forgiven. It helps us appreciate the incredible blessing of forgiveness. But there is more. We not only get to leave *our* sins behind, we get to let *others* leave their sins behind too:

> "Be on your guard! If your brother sins, rebuke him; and if he repents, forgive [*aphiemi*] him. And if he sins against you seven times a day, and returns to you seven times, saying, 'I repent,' forgive [*aphiemi*] him." The apostles said to the Lord, "Increase our faith!"

Luke 17:3-5 NASB

It may not be easy for us to let other people leave *every* one of their sins behind—especially people who are repeat offenders! It is tempting to dredge up their past offenses to prove a point about what they are doing now. But if someone sins and repents, even seven times a day, God expects us to forgive them and let them leave all of their sins behind. (And like the apostles, we say, "Increase our faith!")

Jesus addressed the seriousness of not forgiving others. On one occasion, after teaching his disciples to pray, "Forgive us our debts, as we also have forgiven our debtors,"[15] Jesus added this important lesson:

> For if you forgive [*aphiemi*] others for their transgressions, your heavenly Father will also forgive [*aphiemi*] you. But if

---

15. Matthew 6:12 NASB

you do not forgive [*aphiemi*] others, then your Father will not forgive [*aphiemi*] your transgressions.

Matthew 6:14-15 NASB

Matthew wrote that if we refuse to let other people leave their sins behind, we will not be able to leave ours behind either. Hearing Jesus say this may have resonated with Matthew, because he was a tax collector when Jesus called him to follow. And Jews hated tax collectors because they worked for the Romans and became rich by collecting extra money for themselves. Matthew wanted his fellow Jewish disciples to let him leave his past sins behind too!

In cases where our lives have been forever changed by someone else's sin, we may think, "I can forgive them, but I cannot forget." But it isn't necessary that we forget about someone's sin before we let them leave it behind. We may never forget, but with God's help we can let them leave their sins behind.

Jesus told a parable about a servant who was forgiven a debt he could not pay, but then refused to forgive someone who owed him much less. Jesus explained the serious consequences:

And his lord, moved with anger, handed him over to the torturers until he should repay all that was owed him. "My heavenly Father will also do the same to you, if each of you does not forgive [*aphiemi*] his brother from your heart."

Matthew 18:34-35 NASB

Jesus' words could be interpreted this way: If you don't forgive others from your heart, you will have to pay back all that you owe to God. We have a tendency to think our brother's debt is too big to forgive, yet minimize the size of our own debt to God. But in reality, our debt to God is so big that it is impossible to pay back. Remembering this can help us soften our hearts so we are willing to let others leave their sins behind.

On the cross, Jesus took forgiveness to a whole new level. He forgave people who did not even understand what they had done.

"... Father, forgive [*aphiemi*] them, for they do not know what they are doing..."

Luke 23:34 NASB

I picture the disciples, who heard Jesus say this, first looking intently at Jesus then turning to look at the Roman soldiers and the Jewish rulers, then looking at the expressions on each other's faces. They just heard Jesus ask God to forgive those who were crucifying Him. We see the same heart in Stephen, who prayed while being stoned, "Lord, do not hold this sin against them."[16] God expects us to be like Jesus and Stephen in our willingness to forgive.

At first, the idea of letting other people leave their sins behind may seem more like a "have to" than a "get to," but the fact that we can be free to let others leave their sins behind is one of the many great blessings we have in Christ. Getting to leave our sins behind is a blessing we can *all* rejoice in together!

There is a connection between God's grace (favor) and his forgiveness. Letting us leave all our sins behind is powerful evidence of God's favor. Our being forgiven is "in accordance with the riches of God's grace."[17] A word that will help us understand the connection between forgiveness and God's grace is *charizomai*. The root word of *charizomai* is *charis*, the word translated as "grace."

> **Definition of charizomai:** 1. to give freely as a favor, *give graciously*; 2. to cancel a sum of money that is owed, *cancel*; 3. to show oneself gracious by forgiving wrongdoing, *forgive, pardon*.[18]

Charizomai has to do with showing favor or giving freely. In the NASB, it is translated into the following English words (number of times in parenthesis): forgiven (4), granted (4), forgive (3), forgave (2), forgiving (2), graciously forgave (1), freely give (1), gave (1), given (1),

---

16. Acts 7:60 NASB

17. Ephesians 1:7 NIV

18. <u>BDAG</u>, p. 1078.

bestowed (1), hand (2), freely given (1). Its use in the following verse shows us the heart of God.

> He who did not spare His own Son, but delivered Him over for us all, how will He not also with Him underline{freely give} [*chari-zomai*] us all things? [Emphasis added.]
>
> Romans 8:32 NASB

The gifts God gives to us, including the forgiveness of our sins, are freely given. To communicate this, the NASB translators often used forms of the word "forgive" to translate *charizomai* and sometimes included "graciously" or other words that suggest God's motivation.

> And Jesus answered him, "Simon, I have something to say to you." And he replied, "Say it, Teacher." "A moneylender had two debtors: one owed five hundred denarii, and the other fifty. When they were unable to repay, he graciously forgave [*charizomai*] them both. So which of them will love him more?" Simon answered and said, "I suppose the one whom he forgave [*charizomai*] more." And He said to him, "You have judged correctly." [Emphasis added.]
>
> Luke 7:40-43 NASB

Charizomai describes what the moneylender did about the debts of the men who could not pay. (In place of "graciously forgave," the NIV simply says, "canceled.") From the few details Jesus provided, we learn that the size of the debts of the two men did not matter to the moneylender; he showed his favor to both men. However, the gratitude each man felt for what the moneylender did depended on him realizing how much favor he had received.

The application for us is that God's nature is like that of the moneylender. God is willing to cancel the debt we are unable to pay. The debt in our case is our sin. Then God calls us to have the same heart for each other:

> So, as those who have been chosen of God, holy and beloved, put on a heart of compassion, kindness, humility, gentleness and patience; bearing with one another, and forgiving [*chari-zomai*] each other, whoever has a complaint against anyone;

just as the Lord <u>forgave</u> [*charizomai*] you, so also should you. [Emphasis added.]

Colossians 3:12-13 NASB

We can show favor like God by cancelling the "debts" we think others owe us. We are to forgive them with the same motivation God had for forgiving us. He is loving and kind and graciously forgives us.

We can summarize what it means to be forgiven by saying, we get to leave all of our sins behind. "As far as the east is from the west, so far has he removed our transgressions from us."[19] And God will not hold a grudge for the price Jesus paid to make that possible. God said, "For I will be merciful to their iniquities, and I will remember their sins no more."[20] And finally, if someone sins against us, we are to graciously forgive them and be glad that they can leave their sins behind too.

A Simple Description of Forgiveness:
Getting to leave sins behind

Summary:

To understand the connection between God's grace (favor), mercy (compassion), and forgiveness (leaving our sins behind), consider again the relationship between a father and son. What if a son disobeys his father and knows he deserves to be disciplined? If the father decides to discipline his son, is his favor suddenly in doubt? No, a loving father will discipline his son because of his favor. He wants to help his son learn a valuable lesson.

> Endure hardship as discipline; God is treating you as sons.
> For what son is not disciplined by his father?

Hebrews 12:7 NIV

---

19. Psalms 103:12 NASB
20. Hebrews 8:12 NASB

In the same way, we can be disciplined by God and still have His grace (favor). God does not withhold his favor to punish us—he disciplines us *because of* his favor. That should make us feel more secure rather than less. According to the writer of Hebrews, this is proof that we are legitimate children of God:

> If you are not disciplined (and everyone undergoes discipline), then you are illegitimate children and not true sons.
>
> Hebrews 12:8 NIV

In our father and son example, if the father shows mercy and does not discipline his son, the son may still face consequences. He may get a skinned knee for running when he was told he should walk, or get a speeding ticket when he ignores his father's warnings to observe the speed limits. And so it is with us. We may face consequences if we disobey God, even if God is merciful toward us. We often bring consequences on ourselves. But just like the son, we can still have the favor of God.

How important is forgiveness to the son? Not being disciplined may make the son happy, but what matters most in this relationship is his father's forgiveness. If the father forgives him, he will let him leave his disobedience behind and not hold it against him in the future. But if the father does not forgive him, there will always be a barrier in their relationship. This helps us understand why God sent Jesus to give us a way to leave all of our sins behind.

As we think about the difference between mercy (compassion) and forgiveness, it helps to be aware that God's compassion is evident in more ways than just through his forgiveness. Compassion moves him to offer us relief from all kinds of trials and to meet all kinds of needs. In the example of the father and son, the father may offer his son relief by bandaging a skinned knee. He may even give his son an opportunity to earn the money he needs to pay the fine for speeding. Forgiveness is only one benefit of God's mercy.

When the scriptures were written, the Greek words translated "grace," "mercy" and "forgiveness" were just common, everyday words. But over time, confusion about their meanings has made it more difficult to understand and appreciate God's grace. The word grace, in particular, has taken on meanings that are far different from the way the word was used in the original text. Often grace, mercy and forgiveness are used interchangeably and grace and mercy are confused with salvation.

Soteria, the Greek word translated "salvation," is never translated grace. *Charis*, the only word translated "grace" in the NASB, is never translated salvation or forgiveness. The only word translated "forgiveness" in the NASB is *aphesis*. Lastly, *eleos*, the word translated "mercy" or "compassion," is never translated grace, forgiveness or salvation. I am stressing these facts because clarity helps us understand the scriptures and appreciate who God is and what he has done for us.

In the following chapters, we will look at the many facets of God's grace and all the ways it can impact our lives. As you continue reading, keep these simple descriptions for grace, mercy and forgiveness in mind:

- God's GRACE is His favor.

- MERCY is the compassion to offer relief.

- FORGIVENESS is getting to leave sins behind.

WORKSHEET 1 – Grace, Mercy & Forgiveness

1. How would you explain God's grace to someone?

_____

_____

_____

_____

_____

_____

_____

_____

_____

_____

_____

2. In what ways has God offered you relief?

_____

_____

_____

_____

_____

_____

_____

_____

3. What would help you be more compassionate?

_____

_____

_____

_____

_____

_____

_____

_____

_____

_____

4. Describe what it means to let someone leave their sins behind.

_____

_____

_____

_____

_____

_____

_____

_____

_____

_____

_____

_____

_____

Chapter Notes:

Chapter 2

Grace in the Old Testament

In the previous chapter, we explored the biblical meaning of grace by looking at the use of the Greek word *charis* in the New Testament. Now we will consider two additional New Testament passages where *charis* is used that call our attention to the presence of God's grace in the Old Testament.

> Therefore it says, "God is opposed to the proud but gives grace [*charis*] to the humble."
>
> James 4:6 NASB

> ...All of you, clothe yourselves with humility toward one another, for God is opposed to the proud but gives grace [*charis*] to the humble.
>
> 1 Peter 5:5b NASB

To describe the nature of God's grace, both James and Peter quoted from the Septuagint translation[21] of the following Old Testament passage:

> The curse of the LORD is on the house of the wicked, but He blesses the dwelling of the righteous. Though He scoffs at the scoffers, yet He gives grace [*chen*] to the afflicted.
>
> Proverbs 3:33-34 NASB

---

21.   The Septuagint is the oldest translation of the Hebrew Bible into the Greek language.

The NIV reads, "He gives grace to the humble." The Hebrew word translated "grace" is *chen*. To describe the quality of God represented by the Hebrew word *chen*, both James and Peter used the Greek word *charis*.

> **Definition of *chen*:** 1. grace, charm; 2. favor, popularity, *gives him favor with; cause to obtain favor; to put in favor, to find favor.*[22]

By looking at uses of the word *chen*, we will see how God's grace was displayed in the Old Testament and how it has always been the foundation of man's relationship with Him. *Chen* appears sixty-nine times in the Old Testament. The NASB translates *chen* as "favor" fifty-one times and eight times as "grace." In ten other places, it is translated gracious, graceful, charm, charming, adornment or pleases. Here are two instances where *chen* is translated as "grace:"

> "At that time," declares the Lord, "I will be the God of all the families of Israel, and they shall be My people." Thus says the Lord, "The people who survived the sword found grace [*chen*] in the wilderness— Israel, when it went to find its rest."
>
> Jeremiah 31:1-2 NASB

> For the Lord God is a sun and shield; the Lord gives grace [*chen*] and glory; no good thing does He withhold from those who walk uprightly.
>
> Psalms 84:11 NASB

More often, though, *chen* is translated as "favor."

> Do not let kindness and truth leave you; bind them around your neck, write them on the tablet of your heart so you will find favor [*chen*] and good repute in the sight of God and man.
>
> Proverbs 3:3-4 NASB

---

22.   Koehler, Baumgartner and Stamm's, The Hebrew and Aramaic Lexicon of the Old Testament, (Brill Academic Publishers, 2002) .

Notice that *chen* was used to describe both the favor of men and of God. *Chen* was also the word used to describe Potiphar's initial treatment of Joseph[23] and the way Boaz responded to Ruth.[24] Nehemiah asked for *chen* from King Artaxerxes.[25] Here are some other notable examples where *chen* was translated favor:

Noah: But Noah found favor [*chen*] in the eyes of the LORD.

Genesis 6:8 NASB

Abraham: My Lord, if now I have found favor [*chen*] in Your sight, please do not pass Your servant by.

Genesis 18:3 NASB

Moses: Now therefore, I pray You, if I have found favor [*chen*] in Your sight, let me know Your ways that I may know You, so that I may find favor [*chen*] in Your sight…

Exodus 33:13a NASB

Gideon: So Gideon said to Him, "If now I have found favor [*chen*] in Your sight, then show me a sign that it is You who speak with me."

Judges 6:17 NASB

Noah had God's favor; Abraham and Moses wanted to know if they did; and Gideon went to great lengths to be absolutely sure that he had found favor with God. All of this helps us see that grace is not just a New Testament principle. The Hebrew word *chen*, like *charis*, was a commonly used word that expressed grace or a form of favor. Thus, God's grace can be thought of as His favor in both the Old and New Testaments.

Think about the potential impact of the favor of God in your life. Nothing is more important. But both James and Peter wrote that something as common as pride could keep us from having the favor of God. God gives grace to the humble, but will oppose the proud. In both the

---

23.   Genesis 39:4

24.   Ruth 2:10-13

25.   Nehemiah 2:5

Old and New Testaments, pride has kept men from having a relationship with God. So it would be good to know what God considers being proud. We find out from the context of what James wrote:

> You adulteresses, do you not know that friendship with the world is hostility toward God? Therefore whoever wishes to be a friend of the world makes himself an enemy of God. Or do you think that the Scripture speaks to no purpose: "He jealously desires the Spirit which He has made to dwell in us"? But He gives a greater <u>grace</u> [*charis*]. Therefore it says, "God is opposed to the proud, but gives <u>grace</u> [*charis*] to the humble." [Emphasis added.]

James 4:4-6 NASB

Humility is not just a noble ideal—receiving God's grace (favor) depends on it. And what God considers a lack of humility could be a surprise—wanting a friendship with the world. Striving to fit in with the world will keep us from having a relationship with God. The favor of the world may look attractive and can make us feel good about ourselves, but you cannot have both the favor of the world and the favor of God. Here is one of the clearest warnings in scripture about the dangers of seeking friendship with the world:

> Do not love the world nor the things in the world. If anyone <u>loves the world</u>, the <u>love of the Father is not in him</u>. For all that is in the world, the lust of the flesh and the lust of the eyes and <u>the boastful pride of life</u>, is not from the Father, but <u>is from the world</u>. The world is passing away, and *also* its lusts; but the one who does the will of God lives forever. [Emphasis added.]

1 John 2:15-17 NASB

The pull of our world today is really no different than it was when James wrote, "Friendship with the world is hatred toward God."[26] Only the packaging has changed. Movies, advertisements, television commercials, and even television shows themselves make friendship with the world look exciting and minimize the risks and serious consequences.

---

26. James 4:4 NIV

They send the message that everybody else is having fun, so you should get a piece of the action. But valuing any part of the world more than our relationship with God will keep us from having the favor of God. If we are not careful, even success in things that are good can make us prideful and cause us to boast in ourselves instead of God.

Aware of the dangers of pride, and the challenges his readers were facing, James writes, "Do you not know?" In other words, don't you see what is happening? The lesson for us could not be clearer. If we want the blessings of living our lives in the favor of God, we cannot also try to fit in and be friends with the world. Choosing to be a friend of the world will make us an enemy of God. God has given us fair warning.

The world can feed our pride by making us feel important, and may even provide some other short-term rewards, but the favor of any human—even all the favor in the world—cannot possibly compare with the favor of God.

> But He gives a greater grace. Therefore it says, "God is op-posed to the proud, but gives grace to the humble." [Emphasis added.]
>
> James 4:6 NASB

God gives us "greater grace." Is that what those words really mean? Yes, God gives us greater favor than we can find in the world. And God's favor is worth more than anything the world can even claim to offer!

Men have always had to choose between the favor of the world and the favor of God. Moses is a good example:

> By faith Moses, when he had grown up, refused to be known as the son of Pharaoh's daughter. He chose to be mistreated along with the people of God rather than to enjoy the pleasures of sin for a short time. He regarded disgrace for the sake of Christ as of greater value than the treasures of Egypt, because he was looking ahead to his reward. [Emphasis added.]
>
> Hebrews 11:24-26 NIV

Moses looked past what might be attractive in the short-term and took an eternal view of the purpose of his life. He turned down the opportunity to be treated like a king to be, instead, mistreated and to suffer with God's people. That choice led to forty years of life in the wilderness. Then God called Moses to lead the Israelites out of Egyptian bondage. Despite how it might have looked, Moses had the favor of God. Through Moses' experiences, he would come to enjoy one of the closest relationships anyone has ever had with God.

Here is a brief overview of what Moses faced as the leader of the Israelites: When Pharaoh finally let the Israelites go, they lacked the confidence to stand up to their enemies, so God took them on a route through the desert to avoid the possibility of war with the Philistines. Then when Pharaoh changed his mind and went after the Israelites, the people turned on Moses. Nevertheless, God rescued them by enabling Moses to part the Red Sea, and then used the same waters to destroy Pharaoh's army. In response, the Israelites worshipped God, but after three days in the desert without water, they began grumbling about Moses' leadership. When they complained about being hungry, God fed them with bread and quail from heaven. When they grumbled about being thirsty, God made water come out of a rock. But the Israelites still disobeyed His commands. While Moses was up on Mt. Sinai receiving the new law, the Israelites made a golden calf and declared it to be their god who brought them out of Egypt.[27] In spite of the way God always took care of them and the devotion of Moses as their leader, the people were unfaithful to God.

After the events described above, Moses had the following conversation with God. As you read, keep in mind what Moses had been through to carry out the responsibility God gave him.

> Then Moses said to the LORD, "See, You say to me, 'Bring up this people!' But You Yourself have not let me know whom You will send with me. Moreover, You have said, 'I have known you by name, and you have also found <u>favor</u> [*chen*] in My sight.' "Now therefore, I pray You, if I have found <u>favor</u> [*chen*] in Your sight, <u>let me know Your ways that I may know You,</u> so that I may find <u>favor</u> [*chen*] in Your sight. Consider too, that this nation is Your people." And He

---

27. Exodus 13:17-18; Exodus 14:11-12; Exodus 14:29 – 15:24; Exodus 17:1-7; and Exodus 32:1-4.

said, "My presence shall go with you, and I will give you rest." [Emphasis added.]

...The Lord said to Moses, "I will also do this thing of which you have spoken; for you have found <u>favor</u> [*chen*] in My sight and I have known you by name." [Emphasis added.]

Exodus 33:12-14; 17 NASB

Moses could have asked God for many things. What would you want if you were asked to lead a nation of obstinate people? How about time off to rest, or more wisdom or physical strength? Instead, Moses asked, "Let me know your ways." Moses reaffirmed his deep desire to know God. We see his humility in that request. He was living by his decision to value the favor of God over the favor of the world. God graciously agreed to do what Moses asked. It must have pleased Moses to hear God say that He would be the one to go with him.

Moses was known for his humility.[28] He knew that the strength he needed to lead the Israelites came from God. We also see humility in Noah, Abraham and Gideon, whose success was a result of the favor of God. Humble men are known for what God does through them, despite their limitations. Prideful men, on the other hand, want to be known for what they have accomplished by themselves. It takes a humble man to say, "Teach me your ways and go with me." The prideful say, "Watch me and learn from me."

Throughout the history of man, the proud have thought they could take care of themselves, and placed little or no value on the favor of God. They even acted as if they didn't need it. Consider what happened to King Manasseh:

The Lord spoke to Manasseh and his people, <u>but they paid no attention</u>. So the Lord brought against them the army commanders of the king of Assyria, who took Manasseh prisoner, put a hook in his nose, bound him with bronze shackles and took him to Babylon. [Emphasis added.]

2 Chronicles 33:10-11 NIV

---

28. Numbers 12:3

41

Manasseh had done more evil than the pagan nations that the Israelites saw the Lord destroy; he had filled Jerusalem with blood from one end to the other.[29] And Manasseh was so prideful that he would not listen, even when confronted by the Lord. But when the king of Assyria put a hook in his nose and took him to Babylon, Manasseh finally became humble:

> In his distress he sought the favor of the Lord his God and humbled himself greatly before the God of his fathers. And when he prayed to him, the Lord was moved by his entreaty and listened to his plea; so he brought him back to Jerusalem and to his kingdom. Then Manasseh knew that the Lord is God.
>
> 2 Chronicles 33:12-13 NIV

When Manasseh felt the opposition of God, it humbled him. Then God restored him to his place as king, and Manasseh led the people to worship God. Manasseh's story is a good example of how God opposes the proud, but gives His grace to the humble. He experienced both the opposition of God and his favor.

Final Thoughts:

If we think of God's grace as salvation, and believe (as we should) that salvation can only be ours through Jesus, the idea of Old Testament grace will not make sense. But when the Greek word *charis* and the Hebrew word *chen* are used to describe a quality of God, they are referring to His favor, not salvation. And, as we have seen, there are many Old Testament examples of the grace (favor) of God.

In the next chapter, we will examine the evidence of God's grace in the lives of Noah and Gideon.

---

29. 2 Chronicles 33:9; 2 Kings 21:16

WORKSHEET 2 – Grace in the Old Testament

1. What is the significance of the existence of God's grace in the Old Testament, not just in the New Testament?

_____

_____

_____

_____

_____

_____

2. What favor does the world claim to offer?

_____

_____

_____

_____

_____

_____

3. What does it mean to be a friend of the world?

_____

_____

_____

_____

_____

_____

4. How does God give us more grace (favor) than the world?

_____

_____

_____

_____

_____

_____

_____

_____

_____

_____

5. Why is humility a condition for receiving God's grace (favor)?

_____

_____

_____

_____

_____

_____

_____

_____

_____

_____

Chapter Notes:

Chapter 3

By the Grace of God: Noah & Gideon

Noah and Gideon came from different backgrounds and faced very different challenges, but the favor of God changed both of their lives dramatically. Noah had already lived 500 years when God called him to build the ark. He was a righteous man who walked with God and was a "preacher of righteousness."[30] He stood out to God above everyone else. Gideon, on the other hand, was the youngest of the weakest family in Manasseh and relatively inexperienced when it came to having a relationship with God. We will see different aspects of the *chen* of God in the lives of these men.

Noah (Genesis 6-8):

> But Noah found <u>favor</u> [*chen*] in the eyes of the LORD. These are the records of the generations of Noah. Noah was a righteous man, blameless in his time; Noah walked with God. [Emphasis added.]
>
> Genesis 6:8-9 NASB

In this scripture, the Hebrew word *chen* is translated as "favor." It is easy to see why Noah had God's favor; he was blameless during a time when the earth was corrupt and full of violence.[31] That shows the depth

---

30. 2 Peter 2:5

31. Genesis 6:9,11

of his conviction and his faith in God. So when God was grieved by how wicked man had become, and was ready to destroy everything he had created, he put in motion a plan to save Noah and his family.

> Then God said to Noah, "The end of all flesh has come before Me; for the earth is filled with violence because of them; and behold, I am about to destroy them with the earth. Make for yourself an ark of gopher wood; you shall make the ark with rooms, and shall cover it inside and out with pitch. This is how you shall make it..."
>
> Genesis 6:13-15 NASB

Because God favored Noah, he warned him about the impending destruction, and told him what to do to prepare for it. He gave Noah the exact dimensions and proportions for a 450 foot vessel that would not sink or tip over.[32] The job was so big, it took many decades to complete. Someone watching Noah toil day after day might have thought that either Noah was crazy or that he was being punished. In reality, though, he had been singled out for special treatment. Noah was favored by God. His family would be the only people God saved. Given the options—build the ark or be destroyed—Noah was favored by God!

How would you have felt if you had been Noah and were asked to do something more difficult than anything you had ever done before? I would have had lots of questions: "Why me? How will I know what to do? What will happen if I fail? What's an ark?" It appears, however, that Noah willingly accepted the job. If Noah had any questions or objections, we are not told. One warning from God was all that Noah needed. The writer of Hebrews said this about Noah's faith:

> By faith Noah, when warned about things not yet seen, in holy fear built an ark to save his family. By his faith he condemned the world and became heir of the righteousness that comes by faith.
>
> Hebrews 11:7 NIV

---

32. Genesis 6:15-16

So because of God's favor, Noah knew what would happen long before the rain started to fall. And because Noah obeyed God and built the ark, he was prepared for the flood.

> Then the Lord said to Noah, "Enter the ark, you and all your household, for you alone I have seen to be righteous before Me in this time. You shall take with you of every clean animal by sevens, a male and his female; and of the animals that are not clean two, a male and his female; also of the birds of the sky, by sevens, male and female, to keep offspring alive on the face of all the earth. For after seven more days, I will send rain on the earth forty days and forty nights; and I will blot out from the face of the land every living thing that I have made." Noah did according to all that the Lord had commanded him.
>
> Genesis 7:1-5 NASB

Doing what God told Noah to do took more than just physical energy and determination; it took faith and deep convictions. I imagine that Noah was ridiculed by people who happened to pass by: "Hey, Noah, what's that monstrosity in your back yard? You're building a *what*? For when the water does what?" Noah knew that he had the favor of God, so what people said would not matter. He was determined to please God and take care of his family, so he just kept building the ark. Because Noah listened to God, he was ready when the water came.

> Now Noah was six hundred years old when the flood of water came upon the earth. Then Noah and his sons and his wife and his sons' wives with him entered the ark because of the water of the flood.
>
> Genesis 7:6-7 NASB

When the water was rising, Noah no longer looked foolish. But what can we say about the people who scoffed as they watched Noah build or heard him preach and did not respond? Jesus described their plight like this:

> For in the days before the flood, people were eating and drinking, marrying and giving in marriage, up to the day Noah

entered the ark; and they knew nothing about what would happen until the flood came and took them all away.

Matthew 24:38-39a NIV

The people were not prepared for what happened because they did not seek to know God. Instead, they were busy with life. We are not told, but because Noah was a preacher of righteousness, it seems reasonable to think that Noah would have tried to persuade them.

We learn some important lessons from Noah. Because Noah walked with God and had His favor, he was prepared for the flood. Notice too that walking with God was the way in which Noah found himself in a situation that called for great faith. Noah had the favor of God, but it still took faith to do what he did.

Similarly, God will never let us take faith out of the equation! We too must walk with God and faithfully obey what he tells us, even if it is something we have never done before. God promises to live with us, and walk among us and be our God,[33] so his favor will surely be enough. "For if God . . .did not spare the ancient world when he brought the flood on its ungodly people, but protected Noah, a preacher of righteousness, and seven others . . . then the Lord knows how to rescue godly men from trials."[34]

Finally, the grace (favor) of God seldom affects only one person; it will often impact the lives of other people. Because Noah had the favor of God, his family enjoyed an obvious blessing. We don't know how they felt during all those years when Noah was building the ark. Hopefully they were eager to help Noah, but I assume that when the waters started to rise, they were grateful for Noah's faith!

Building the ark was a difficult and time-consuming project, but by God's grace, Noah had what he needed to succeed. By God's grace, we too can be prepared. Here are some examples of what that means:

---

33. 2 Corinthians 6:16b NIV

34. 2 Peter 2:4-9a NIV

> His divine power has given us everything we need for life and godliness through our knowledge of him who called us by his own glory and goodness.
>
> 2 Peter 1:3 NIV

> All Scripture is God-breathed and is useful for teaching, rebuking, correcting and training in righteousness, so that the man of God may be thoroughly equipped for every good work.
>
> 2 Timothy 3:16-17 NIV

By God's favor, we have his word to read and apply. He tells us how to build a relationship with him. He also tells us that taking a stand on his behalf will not be popular. People may look at our lives and think what we are building is foolish and a waste of time. But we must be faithful and obedient to God's word and build anyway.

Noah stood out to God above everyone in his time, and is remembered for his incredible faith. But what about someone who did not stand out at all? Next we will look at the impact of the favor of God in the life of Gideon

Gideon (Judges 6-8):

Gideon, in his own words, was the youngest in the family that was the least in Manasseh.[35] (The NIV reads, "weakest in Manasseh.") Gideon did not have a reputation for great accomplishments and had little confidence in himself.

Chapter 5 of Judges ends with the statement: "Then the land had peace for forty years." Chapter 6 begins with: "Again the Israelites did evil in the eyes of the Lord." What happened? The Israelites quit trusting God. They turned away from obeying God's commandments, and had begun to live like the Amorites. So God stopped protecting them from their enemies. Then, when the Israelites were oppressed by the Midianites, instead of turning to God, they sought protection by hiding in caves.

---

35. Judges 6:15 NASB

This went on for seven years before they finally cried out to God. Then God sent a prophet to tell them what they needed to hear.[36] To paraphrase, the prophet said, "I brought you out of Egypt; I drove out your enemies; I gave you their land; and I told you not to worship their gods, but you did not listen." In God's eyes, the Israelites had stopped seeking His favor, and were seeking the favor of the gods of the Amorites. But when the Israelites finally cried out to God, he set in motion a plan to help them. He sent an angel to help Gideon discover something he would not have found out on his own—he had God's favor and was His choice to lead the Israelites in battle against the Midianites.

The exchange between Gideon and the angel of the Lord was interesting. The angel made two simple points: (1) the Lord is with you, and (2) you are a mighty warrior. Gideon was clever enough to thresh wheat in a winepress to avoid being seen by the Midianites,[37] but he did not think of himself as mighty in any way. Gideon then began to question God's concern for the Israelites:

> "But sir," Gideon replied, "if the Lord is with us, why has all this happened to us? Where are all his wonders that our fathers told us about when they said, 'Did not the Lord bring us up out of Egypt?' But now the Lord has abandoned us and put us into the hand of Midian." The Lord turned to him and said, "Go in the strength you have and save Israel out of Midian's hand. Am I not sending you?" "But Lord," Gideon asked, "how can I save Israel? My clan is the weakest in Manasseh, and I am the least in my family." The Lord answered, "I will be with you, and you will strike down all the Midianites together." Gideon replied, "<u>If now I have found favor [*chen*] in your eyes, give me a sign that it is really you talking to me.</u>" [Emphasis added.]

> Judges 6:13-17 NIV

Gideon said, "If you are with us, why are we in this mess?" To which the Lord replied, "Go in the strength you have," Then when

---

36. Judges 6:7-10

37. Judges 6:11

Gideon responded with "What strength?" The Lord said, "I am still sending you."

God had not abandoned the Israelites; they had abandoned God. And to make matters worse, they blamed God for withholding his miracles. In essence, they were complaining about not having the favor of God when they were not seeking it. And when God tried to send Gideon to the rescue, Gideon made excuses for not wanting to go. He did not think he was up to the task.

The lesson for us, though, is not about Gideon's excuses, but about what we can accomplish with God's favor, and how far God will go to show us that we have it. Like Gideon, we have to realize that God is not being unfair when he calls us to go in the strength we have and rely on Him for what we need. God wants us to know that if we trust and obey him, he will show us his favor. We do not need to fight our spiritual battles on our own.

Although Gideon struggled in his faith, he was interested enough in what the Lord said to make him want to investigate. He asked, "If now I have found favor [*chen*] in your eyes, give me a sign that it is really you talking to me."[38] Gideon devised a way to get proof. The Lord did what Gideon asked, and gave him proof of His favor by making fire consume the offering Gideon prepared. Gideon suddenly realized he was talking to the angel of the Lord and was terrified. Gideon had problems, but he still had respect for God's power. Then God said, "Peace! Do not be afraid. You are not going to die."[39] Hearing this good news, Gideon worshiped God!

Later that night, God appeared to Gideon again. To help Gideon take the next step, God called him to have the courage to destroy his father's altar to Baal and cut down the Asherah pole[40] beside it. Gideon

---

38.   Judges 6:17 NIV

39.   Judges 6:19-24 NIV

40.   A cultic object representing the presence of the Canaanite goddess Asherah. (W. E. Vine, <u>Vine's Expository Dictionary of Old Testament and New Testament Words</u>, WORD*search* 8.0.2.40 (WORD*search* Corp, 2008). Hereafter cited as Vine.)

was fearful—he went at night with ten servants for moral support—but he found the courage to do it.[41]

Gideon began assembling an army to fight the Midianites, but he still needed more assurance, so he asked for another sign. If you make the fleece wet and the ground dry then I will know." After God did what he had asked, Gideon said, "Now if you do just the opposite, I will really know."[42] Gideon tested God a total of three times. Was that okay? I might have been impatient, but not God. God made it very clear to Gideon: "I am with you." By now, Gideon surely knew he had God's favor.

Even as he asked for more proof of God's favor, Gideon was rallying an army of 32,000 men to fight the Midianites. Gideon was concerned about being too weak. But for God's purposes, Gideon's army was too strong. The tension must have been building as Gideon watched God reduce the size of his army from 32,000 to 300 men.[43] God made sure that Gideon could never attribute his impending victory to his own strength.

Eventually, Gideon's army of 300 was ready. During the night, God told Gideon to go down against the Midianite camp, for "I am going to give it into your hands."[44] Then without being asked, God offered Gideon another opportunity to know that He was with him. God told Gideon that if he was still afraid to attack, he could take his servant and go down near the camp and listen to what the men there were saying. Gideon arrived at the camp just as a man was telling his friend about his dream:

---

41. Judges 6:25-32
42. Judges 6:34-40
43. Judges 7:1-7
44. Judges 7:9 NIV

"A round loaf of barley bread came tumbling into the Midianite camp. It struck the tent with such force that the tent overturned and collapsed."

His friend responded, "This can be nothing other than the sword of Gideon son of Joash, the Israelite. <u>God has given the Midianites and the whole camp into his hands</u>."

When Gideon heard the dream and its interpretation, he worshiped God. He returned to the camp of Israel and called out, "Get up! The Lord has given the Midianite camp into your hands." [Emphasis added.]

Judges 7:13b-15 NIV

What Gideon overheard gave him confidence. The first thing he did was worship God. Then he was ready to attack! Gideon now believed that he had God's favor. That night God gave Gideon and his men a great victory.

Gideon was not the obvious person to lead the Israelites into battle; he was weak and afraid. But when he became convinced that he had God's favor, he led the Israelites to conquer the vast Midianite army. Even Gideon's enemies realized that he had God's favor.

Gideon used unconventional weapons that lacked any visible signs of power, but when he went with the strength he had, God made up the difference, and a seven-year-old battle came to an end. Despite what we might call a slow start, Gideon was recognized by the writer of Hebrews for his faith.

And what more shall I say? I do not have time to tell about <u>Gideon</u>, Barak, Samson, Jephthah, David, Samuel and the prophets, who through faith conquered kingdoms, administered justice, and gained what was promised; who shut the mouths of lions, quenched the fury of the flames, and escaped the edge of the sword; whose <u>weakness was turned</u>

to strength; and who <u>became powerful in battle and routed foreign armies</u>. [Emphasis added.]

Hebrews 11:32-34 NIV

Proverbs 13:15 tells us that "Good understanding wins favor [*chen*], but the way of the unfaithful is hard." Living in caves for seven years would be hard, but when the Israelites finally cried out, God quickly showed his favor. God sent a prophet and raised up Gideon out of his weakness and fear. God used an ordinary man to inspire the Israelites to trust Him, and to help them stand up to the Midianites.

Here is a note to parents: Your children also need to understand and appreciate the favor of God. Bring God into everything you do, and let them see the importance of His favor in your life. Consider what a son of Israelite parents would have concluded if his family was one of those hiding in caves. A ten-year-old boy who went into the caves with his parents would be seventeen when victory finally came. For seven years, he would have watched as the adults in his life failed to trust God. From what Gideon said, they may even have been complaining that God had deserted them. What picture would this teenager have had of God? How would he think God's people should act? Make sure your children see your devotion to God and the results of his favor in your life. This will help them build a foundation for their faith.

Finally, many of us can relate to Gideon. We often do not feel up to the task before us. We can even justify our lack of faith. For example, we might think, "If I saw an angel of God burn up my food, I would have more faith too." But many of us have seen the power of God in our lives again and again, and are still reluctant to step out on faith. Even if our faith is weak, we must turn to God and not somewhere else (or another person) for strength. And we must not let our weaknesses define who we are. Looking at our weaknesses instead of God can cause us to miss the greatest source of strength in our lives. It is unlikely that we will need Gideon's unorthodox military techniques, but we can win our spiritual battles if we go in the strength we have, and let God make up the difference.

Gideon discovered the importance of the favor of God, and found out first-hand about the miracles he'd only heard about before. When he finally became convinced, he went in faith and God blessed his efforts. In the end, Gideon proved to be the "mighty warrior" that the angel of the Lord said he was. But he never would have discovered that or accomplished what he did without the favor of God.

Summary:

The stories of Noah and Gideon give us inspiring examples of the favor of God and the impact it can have in someone's life. Noah was able to save his family and preserve mankind. Gideon was able to rescue God's people from a powerful enemy, and experience firsthand the wonders of God. Although Noah and Gideon came from very different circumstances, they were both blessed by God's favor. With God's favor, they accomplished things they never would have accomplished on their own. The same is true for us. Our lives will be changed if we trust God and respond faithfully to the favor he shows us.

WORKSHEET 3 – By the Grace of God: Noah & Gideon

1. How was Noah's life changed by the favor of God?

_____

_____

_____

_____

2. What changed Gideon's view of himself?

_____

_____

_____

_____

3. What life-changing opportunities have you had because of the favor of God?

_____

_____

_____

_____

4. How does the favor of God make a difference when you feel weak or inadequate?

_____

_____

_____

_____

_____

Chapter Notes:

Chapter 4

Paul: A Lesson in Grace, Mercy & *Forgiveness*

To learn more about grace, mercy and forgiveness, we will use the Apostle Paul as a case study. His writings give us detailed information about his life and what he believed. He wrote and taught more about God's grace than anyone else in the New Testament.

Have you given much thought to *when* you first had the benefit of God's grace in your life? When did you first experience the mercy of God? Does one come before the other? Are both necessary before a person can be forgiven? In this chapter, we will use Paul's life as an example. Take a moment and reflect on the following questions about Paul's life:

1. From what you know about Paul, when did he first receive the grace of God?

2. When did Paul receive mercy from God?

3. When were Paul's sins forgiven?

When did Paul first receive the grace of God?

We can find plenty of evidence of the grace of God in Paul's life, but at what point did it begin? Consider what Paul wrote about himself to the churches in Galatia:

> For you have heard of my former manner of life in Judaism, how I used to persecute the church of God beyond measure and tried to destroy it; and I was advancing in Judaism beyond many of my contemporaries among my countrymen, being more extremely zealous for my ancestral traditions. But when God, <u>who had set me apart even from my mother's womb and called me through His grace</u> [*charis*], was pleased to reveal His Son in me so that I might preach Him among the Gentiles… [Emphasis added.]
>
> Galatians 1:13-16 NASB

When Paul wrote this, he was a mature Christian looking back on his life. He concluded that God had favored him from birth by setting him apart for his eventual purpose. Paul has a point. As a Jew, he was educated under Gamaliel, who was a member of the Sanhedrin and a teacher of the law held in high honor among all the people.[45] Being thoroughly trained in the Jewish law would prove useful to Paul in his later ministry. Likewise, Paul's Roman citizenship would eventually open doors for him to preach to the most powerful Romans of his day.[46] By God's grace (favor), Paul was well prepared to preach Jesus to kings, to the sons of Israel and to the Gentiles.[47]

As a young man, though, Paul used his position and influence to persecute Christians. He attempted to destroy the church. So how could such a person have God's grace? Ironically, using Paul to preach the gospel was part of God's plan. Through his grace, God set Paul apart from birth and was preparing him for a role that would come later. Then, when the time came, God was pleased to reveal Jesus to Paul, so that he could preach boldly among Jews and Gentiles. By favoring Paul and choosing him for this important role, God gave us a powerful example of the life-changing impact of knowing Jesus.

Still, the idea that Paul had God's grace from birth may be difficult to accept. Our reaction depends on our understanding of God's grace. For example, if we confuse grace with salvation, it will make no

---

45. Acts 22:3; Acts 5:34

46. Acts 26, Festus & King Agrippa; Acts 27:24, Caesar

47. Acts 9:15

sense at all. But remember that the simple description of God's grace is his favor, and God's grace and salvation are very different.[48] One can experience the grace (favor) of God, but not have salvation. That is what happened to Paul. By his grace, God was preparing Paul for a totally unexpected assignment. The way Paul chose to explain such an unlikely turn of events was that he had God's favor from birth. He had been set apart by God from his mother's womb.

God's plan for Paul's life began to unfold as he traveled on the road to Damascus.

> As he was traveling, it happened that he was approaching Damascus, and suddenly a light from heaven flashed around him; and he fell to the ground and heard a voice saying to him, "Saul, Saul, why are you persecuting Me?" And he said, "Who are You, Lord?" And He said, "I am Jesus whom you are persecuting, but get up and enter the city, and it will be told you what you must do." The men who traveled with him stood speechless, hearing the voice but seeing no one. Saul got up from the ground, and though his eyes were open, he could see nothing; and leading him by the hand, they brought him into Damascus. And he was three days without sight, and neither ate nor drank.
>
> Acts 9:3-9 NASB

What an unforgettable experience! Paul (then known as Saul) finds out that the man named Jesus whom he had been persecuting, was actually the Lord. He was knocked to the ground and lost his eyesight in the process. Paul had been trying to serve God whole-heartedly, but found out how horribly misguided he had been. Then, as instructed, Paul's companions led him to Damascus, where he waited in darkness without food or water. At this point he did not know if he would ever be able to see again. He knew only that he must wait to be told what to do.

---

48. *Charis*, the only Greek word translated as "grace," is never translated "salvation" and *soteria*, the Greek word translated as "salvation," is never translated "grace."

Ananias, a Christian, and the man chosen by God to tell Paul what he must do, understandably did not want to go anywhere near a man with Paul's reputation for persecuting the church:

> But Ananias answered, "Lord, I have heard from many about this man, how much harm he did to Your saints at Jerusalem; and here he has authority from the chief priests to bind all who call on Your name." But the Lord said to him, "<u>Go, for he is a chosen instrument of Mine, to bear My name before the Gentiles and kings and the sons of Israel;</u>" [Emphasis added.]
>
> Acts 9:13-15 NASB

So Ananias, whom Paul would expect to be running away, courageously entered the house where Paul was staying and delivered this life-changing message:

> …"Brother Saul, the Lord Jesus, who appeared to you on the road by which you were coming, has sent me so that you may regain your sight and be filled with the Holy Spirit." And immediately there fell from his eyes something like scales, and he regained his sight, and he got up and was baptized; and he took food and was strengthened.
>
> Acts 9:17b-19a NASB

What happened next would totally surprise everyone, except God.

> …and immediately he began to proclaim Jesus in the synagogues, saying, "He is the Son of God." All those hearing him continued to be amazed, and were saying, "Is this not he who in Jerusalem destroyed those who called on this name, and who had come here for the purpose of bringing them bound before the chief priests?" But Saul kept increasing in strength and confounding the Jews who lived at Damascus by proving that this Jesus is the Christ.
>
> Acts 9:20-22 NASB

If you were looking for someone who could preach Jesus to the Gentiles, a Jew who had devoted his life to persecuting Christians would not even be considered. In fact, Paul might be the last person

Ananias would have expected to be chosen. But Paul was the Lord's "chosen instrument" to proclaim His name to Gentiles, to kings and the sons of Israel. Paul knew he was a most unlikely choice. He wrote, "The grace of our Lord was poured out on me abundantly, along with the faith and love that are in Christ Jesus." [49] God's grace (favor) had to be abundant for Paul to be the one chosen.

In the previous chapters, we saw that God showed his favor to Gideon and Noah. We would expect Noah to have God's favor, but not expect God to choose Gideon. God favored Paul in an unexpected way too. In an interesting twist, God helped him see the truth by first making him blind. God's grace (favor) can work in our lives in ways that we do not expect or understand, and we can have God's favor before we even realize what he is doing.

Another conclusion we can draw from Paul's example is that we can have God's grace before we have salvation. Understanding this can open our eyes to see God's grace in ways we might otherwise overlook. Can you look back on your life and see how God favored you, perhaps long before you saw your need for him? You may see God's favor through the person who reached out to you and led you to Christ, or perhaps it was through your parents or grandparents, who gave you good training and a godly example to follow. The possibilities of how God has shown his favor to you are many.

When did Paul receive mercy from God?

Paul must have been asked many times why he, of all people, had been chosen by God for his special role. Why would a persecutor of Christians be chosen to preach Jesus to anybody? Here is Paul's answer to that question:

> ...even though I was formerly a blasphemer and a persecutor and a violent aggressor. Yet I was <u>shown mercy</u> [*eleeo*] because I acted ignorantly in unbelief; and the <u>grace</u> [*charis*] of our Lord was more than abundant, with the faith and love which are found in Christ Jesus. It is a trustworthy statement, deserving full acceptance, that Christ Jesus came into the

---

49. 1 Timothy 1:14 NIV

world to save sinners, among whom I am foremost of all. Yet for this reason I <u>found mercy</u> [*eleeo*], so that in me as the foremost, Jesus Christ might demonstrate His perfect patience as an example for those who would believe in Him for eternal life. [Emphasis added.]

1 Timothy 1:13-16 NASB

Paul looked back on a dark time in his life, and described himself using words such as *violent* and *persecutor*. Calling himself a blasphemer showed that he realized he had been opposing God. But despite everything in Paul's past, God showed him mercy. Remember that the simple description for mercy is "the compassion to offer relief." God felt compassion for Paul.

As a point of clarification, receiving God's compassion (mercy) does not mean Paul was forgiven. *Eleeo*, the word translated "mercy" two times in 1 Timothy 1:13-16, is from the root word *eleos*, the word most often translated "mercy" or "compassion." *Eleeo* means "to be greatly concerned about someone in need, *have compassion/mercy/ pity*."[50] Neither *eleos* nor *eleeo* are translated "grace," "forgiveness" or "salvation" anywhere in the NASB New Testament.

As we established earlier, Paul realized that he had God's grace from birth. Now we understand that God showed Paul mercy by letting him live while he was persecuting Christians. Of note was the time God showed Paul mercy by letting him walk away from the stoning of Stephen. And just before beginning his trip to Damascus, Paul was still "breathing threats and murder against the disciples of the Lord."[51] God showed Paul mercy when Christians would not have imagined it was possible. God showed Paul mercy before Paul had any idea that he needed it.

God's mercy for Paul was amazing. If I were in the position of God, and knew that Paul had been threatening my children, I would have stopped him at my earliest opportunity. But that is not what God did. Instead, he showed Paul compassion and waited for the right time to convert him to Jesus and put him to work, defending instead of

---

50. <u>BDAG</u>, p.315,
51. Acts 9:1 NASB

attacking the gospel. We see God's incredible patience and how far he will go to show mercy. As we think about all of this, it would be good for us to consider these words from Isaiah:

> "For my thoughts are not your thoughts, neither are your ways my ways," declares the Lord. "As the heavens are higher than the earth, so are my ways higher than your ways and my thoughts than your thoughts."
>
> Isaiah 55:8-9 NIV

Without God's mercy, Paul's life could not have been transformed. More specifically, if God had withheld his mercy until Paul figured it out on his own, it is unlikely that Paul would ever have become a Christian. But the best answer to the question of why God showed mercy to a man who opposed Him can be seen in what came about as a result. Paul became living proof of God's mercy. Think about the example this has been to the generations of sinners who have come after him. There is hope. If God had compassion for Paul, we should never doubt His compassion for us.

Mercy begins with an emotion that moves one to take action to offer relief. When God watched Paul persecute Christians, His heart must have ached for Paul. God was not just tolerating Paul; God felt compassion and longed to heal his soul. The same is true for us. God offers us the same kind of compassion.

When were Paul's sins forgiven?

If we are willing to take Paul's word for it, the answer is easy. We can read the answer in Paul's testimony and defense of his ministry after he was arrested in Jerusalem. According to Paul, here is what Ananias told him to do after three days of waiting in Damascus:

> A certain Ananias, a man who was devout by the standard of the Law, and well spoken of by all the Jews who lived there, came to me, and standing near said to me, "Brother Saul, receive your sight!" And at that very time I looked up at him. And he said, "The God of our fathers has appointed you to know His will and to see the Righteous One and to hear an

utterance from His mouth. For you will be a witness for Him to all men of what you have seen and heard. Now why do you delay? <u>Get up and be baptized, and wash away your sins, calling on His name</u>." [Emphasis added.]

Acts 22:12-16 NASB

Paul had already made three missionary journeys when he gave this testimony in Jerusalem, but he still remembered how his sins were forgiven. It appears that Ananias said only a few words, but the message got through to Paul. It transformed his life. Speaking for God, Ananias told Paul to be baptized and wash away his sins, calling on Christ's name.

Picture how this message would have impacted Paul. For three days he could not see and did not eat. That gave him time to contemplate his sin and his failure in his efforts to serve God. Paul clearly had missed the mark. Then he learned that he could have his sins forgiven. He was told to do the very thing he had persecuted others for doing, perhaps a few days earlier.

Paul was baptized and left all of his sins behind him. Then he immediately went into the synagogues to teach. Paul went from persecuting people who professed to know Jesus to powerfully proclaiming Jesus himself. It was a complete 180-degree turn. He baffled the Jews by using the Jewish law to prove that Jesus was the Christ. His Jewish heritage and education under Gamaliel came in handy. This was the beginning of a ministry that would have an impact on generations to come.

Consider for a moment how God must have felt. He and Paul were finally working together. And Paul was finally freed from his sins. Not only was Paul saved, he was spreading the good news of Jesus to countless others. There must have been great rejoicing in heaven.

God showed Paul grace (favor) from birth, and had compassion (mercy) for Paul on countless occasions, but Paul still needed to be forgiven of his sins. Paul said that this happened when he was baptized. He described God's purpose for baptism like this:

> Therefore we have been buried with Him through baptism into death, so that as Christ was raised from the dead through the glory of the Father, so we too might walk in newness of life. For if we have become united with Him in the likeness of His death, certainly we shall also be in the likeness of His resurrection, knowing this, that our old self was crucified with Him, in order that our body of sin might be done away with, so that we would no longer be slaves to sin; for he who has died is freed from sin.

> Romans 6:4-7 NASB

Paul had been freed from his sins. He explained that baptism symbolizes our spiritual death, burial and resurrection, and that those who have died with Christ are no longer slaves to sin. In the following passage, Paul explained the connection between being saved from our sins and God's grace and mercy. Keep Paul's experience in mind as you consider this passage. To give you perspective, try substituting the word "favor" for "grace" and "compassion" for "mercy" as you read:

> But God, being rich in mercy [compassion], because of His great love with which He loved us, even when we were dead in our transgressions, made us alive together with Christ (<u>by grace [favor] you have been saved</u>), and raised us up with Him, and seated us with Him in the heavenly places in Christ Jesus, so that in the ages to come He might <u>show the surpassing riches of His grace</u> [favor] in kindness toward us in Christ Jesus. For <u>by grace [favor] you have been saved through faith</u>; and that not of yourselves, it is the gift of God; not as a result of works, so that no one may boast. For we are His workmanship, created in Christ Jesus for good works, which God prepared beforehand so that we would walk in them. [Emphasis added.]

> Ephesians 2:4-10 NASB

In this passage, Paul first explained that our salvation is the result of God's favor. By providing a way for us to be saved, God showed us his amazing favor. But to be clear, remember that God showed favor to Paul long before he was saved. By God's favor we *can* be saved, but having God's favor does not mean that we *are* saved.

Second, Paul learned from personal experience that God is rich in mercy. Because of his great love, God showed Paul compassion, even before Paul knew that he needed it. Paul received mercy many times before he finally was baptized for the forgiveness of his sins in Damascus.

Third, we must understand that we are saved through faith, not because we did something to earn it. Paul was a perfect example of being saved by his faith and not by works. His works had been in direct opposition to Jesus. But at last he put his faith in Jesus and called on Jesus' name in baptism. There is no way Paul ever could have felt that he had earned his forgiveness by works. It was a gift from God.

Summary:

Our case study of Paul shows the following:

1. Grace:

God's grace was working in Paul's life long before his sins were forgiven. In fact, in spite of the way Paul had unknowingly worked against God, Paul believed that God favored him from birth.

2. Mercy:

God showed Paul mercy many times throughout his life, even on occasions when he was violently persecuting the church.

3. Forgiveness:

Paul said his sins were forgiven at his baptism. His baptism represented his death, burial and resurrection. In Paul's mind there was no doubt when he was forgiven, and no doubt that he left all his sins behind. As evidence of the latter, he told Timothy that he served God with a clear conscience.[52]

---

52.   2 Timothy 1:3

There are great benefits to realizing that we can have God's grace and mercy before our salvation. First, if our understanding is that we first received mercy and grace at the moment we were saved, we will miss the depth of God's compassion and the way his favor has been and is now at work in our lives. Second, when we sin as a Christian, Satan will try to get us to believe that God's grace depends on our goodness and to have doubts about God's grace and mercy in our lives. That will discourage us and make repenting seem more difficult. But if we understand that we had God's grace (favor) and mercy (compassion) long before we became Christians, we will know that we did not earn it then and cannot earn it now. It was a gift then and it is a gift now. Understanding this will motivate us to repent quickly so we can be close to God.

WORKSHEET 4 - Paul: A Lesson in Grace, Mercy & Forgiveness

1. What is the difference between grace and mercy?

_____

_____

_____

2. As you look back on your life, even before you became a Christian, do you see how God showed you favor? If so, describe?

_____

_____

_____

_____

_____

_____

3. How does it impact you to see how God favored you, even before you were saved?

_____

_____

_____

_____

4. What is the difference between mercy and forgiveness?

_____

_____

_____

_____

Chapter Notes:

_____

_____

_____

_____

_____

_____

_____

_____

_____

_____

_____

_____

_____

_____

_____

_____

_____

_____

_____

_____

_____

_____

_____

_____

_____

Chapter 5

Grace, Faith & Obedience

In the Bible, God makes clear what he wants for us, but he gives us the freedom to choose what we want. We can rely on the favor of God and obey his commands, or ignore God and go after the favor of the world. Or even worse, we can try to live somewhere in the middle.[53]

What does it take to please God? Does his grace cover what we do not do? Some say that all you have to do is believe, others say obedience is what shows we have faith. What is the truth? To answer these questions, we need to consider three foundational principles that we find throughout God's word.

Grace has always been.

Statements such as "You are not under law, but under grace"[54] can leave us with the impression that grace did not exist until after the arrival of Jesus. But as we have already seen in earlier chapters, God's grace also existed before and during the time of the Jewish law. Gideon, who lived his entire life under the law, accomplished great things by the favor of God. Moses, who lived both before and during the law, experienced the favor of God, as did Abraham, who had God's grace long before

---

53. Revelations 3:15-16

54. Romans 6:14

there was a Jewish law. In fact, God's grace was the reason He promised Abraham that he would bless all nations through his descendants:

> For if the inheritance depends on the law, then it no longer depends on a promise; but <u>God in his grace gave it to Abraham</u> through a promise. [Emphasis added.]
>
> Galatians 3:18 NIV

Going back in time even further, God's grace was the reason Noah knew how to save his family from the flood, and why Adam and Eve were so well cared for in Eden. God's grace existed before time began![55] Graciousness is a quality of God, and he does not change.[56] God's grace may seem more obvious in the New Testament because we see God's grace in person—Jesus, the fullness of His grace[57]—but God's grace has always been.

The following statements show why it is important to understand that God's grace has always been. Knowing this gives us a clearer picture of God's grace. These statements build on what we have covered in the previous chapters, and dispel common misconceptions about grace:

- Grace is a quality of God. It is not just a gift He gives us; it is who He is. God is gracious.

- Men have experienced God's favor since time began.

- We can experience God's grace long before we have salvation.

- Receiving God's grace is not a onetime occurrence; we should be mindful of God's favor every day.

---

55. 2 Timothy 1:9 NIV

56. James 1:17 NIV

57. John 1:16-17 NIV

Understanding these points should cause us to look for ways that God has shown us his favor in the past, and motivate us to value his favor more than anything else we could have or be tempted by today.

Faithfulness to God has always been necessary.

The writer of Hebrews defined faith as being sure of what we hope for and certain of what we do not see,[58] then he lifted up men and women who fit that description. Noah, for example, could not see the water, but for years kept building the ark. Gideon gained the confidence to attack a powerful enemy with an ill-equipped band of 300 men. Abraham was willing to go to a place he had not seen.[59] Even when he and Sarah were childless, Abraham believed that his children would be as numerous as the stars.[60]

There were others, though, who lacked faith and had a far different experience. The children of Israel, for example, did not benefit from the message they heard because they did not combine it with faith.[61] They escaped from a life of slavery in Egypt and made it to the border of a land filled with milk and honey, only to turn back because of the obstacles. They did not trust God to fulfill his promises and help them win any battles they might face.[62]

There is no way around our need for faithfulness, and there are no shortcuts to growing in faith. Without faithful decisions and faithful responses to trials, the life God calls us to live will either seem like too much to expect or a burden we have no choice but to bear. Even people who have overcome big obstacles in the past can lose their faith and decide to leave God. That is why the writer of Hebrews warned us that unresolved doubts will eventually cause us to turn away from God.[63]

---

58. Hebrews 11:1 NIV

59. Genesis 12:1-4

60. Genesis 15:6

61. Hebrews 4:1-2 NIV

62. Numbers 13 and 14

63. Hebrews 3:12

Therefore, it is good to examine how faithful we are, and do whatever is necessary to strengthen our faith. It is naïve and even dangerous to take our faithfulness for granted, or assume that we will be faithful in the future because we have been faithful in the past. Our relationship with God and living by faith should be our top priority.

> And without faith it is impossible to please God, because anyone who comes to him must believe that he exists and that he rewards those who earnestly seek him.
>
> Hebrews 11:6 NIV

Faithfulness is absolutely necessary for us to please God. Sadly, though, we can know what Hebrews 11:6 says and even be able to quote it, but still act like we think there is another way to please God. The Pharisees and the teachers of the law, for example, mistakenly thought that their acts of righteousness pleased God. Imagine their surprise when Jesus rebuked them for their lack of faith and their failure to show mercy. They were careful to tithe on something as tiny as spices, but neglected more important matters like faithfulness.[64] They focused more on keeping the law than on being faithful to God. Jesus warned them and called them to change their ways.

It is good that we are inspired by men and women of great faith, like those listed in Hebrews 11. But if we are not careful, we can hold them up for their faith, but then hold ourselves to a lower standard. God calls us to live by faith too.

God has always expected obedience.

From the beginning, man has struggled with obeying God. In the Garden of Eden, Adam and Eve had the full attention and favor of God, and the freedom to do anything except eat from the tree of the knowledge of good and evil. But even Eden did not satisfy Eve. Thinking that God must be somehow holding out on her, Eve fell for Satan's lie and ate the forbidden fruit. And Adam, who apparently was

---

64. Matthew 23:23

more concerned about enjoying the favor of Eve than the favor of God, disobeyed God's direct command and ate too. Adam put his relationship with Eve ahead of obeying God. From that day forward, man has continued to sin.

> Therefore, just as sin entered the world through one man, and death through sin, and in this way death came to all men, because all sinned.
>
> Romans 5:12 NIV

Adam and Eve disobeyed God's only command, and not trusting Him led to their sin. And there were long-term consequences as a result of Adam's sin that did not end until Jesus died on the cross. What happened to Adam and Eve should be a wake-up call for us. They lived in a perfect place. If we think we need something else before we can obey, we are deceived. Having more blessings will not make it easier for us to trust and obey God. If anything, we will be more tempted to put our trust in the things around us.

Throughout the Old Testament, men and women struggled with obedience to God. Some obeyed fully, some partially obeyed, and some completely disobeyed. Abraham was known for his obedience to God. Perhaps the best-known example was when he listened to God and was ready to offer his son Isaac as a sacrifice. Here is what the Lord said to Abraham in response:

> ...Your descendants will take possession of the cities of their enemies, and through your offspring all nations on earth will be blessed, because you have obeyed [*shama*] me.
>
> Genesis 22:17b-18 NIV

The Hebrew word translated "obey" is *shama*. Basically, this verb means to hear with one's ears.[65] *Shama* is translated "listen" or forms of the word "hear" hundreds of times, and 81 times as "obey." God blessed Abraham because he listened and then obeyed what he heard.

Next, consider what happened to King Saul, who chose to partially obey. God told him to completely destroy the Amalekites and their

---

65. Vine.

possessions, but he did not listen. He rationalized that incomplete obedience would be okay. The Prophet Samuel took King Saul to task:

> "Why did you not obey [*shama*] the LORD? Why did you pounce on the plunder and do evil in the eyes of the LORD?"
>
> "But I did obey [*shama*] the LORD," Saul said. "I went on the mission the LORD assigned me. I completely destroyed the Amalekites and brought back Agag their king. The soldiers took sheep and cattle from the plunder, the best of what was devoted to God, in order to sacrifice them to the LORD your God at Gilgal."
>
> But Samuel replied: "Does the LORD delight in burnt offerings and sacrifices as much as in obeying [*shama*] the voice of the LORD? To obey [*shama*] is better than sacrifice, and to heed is better than the fat of rams."
>
> 1 Samuel 15:19-22 NIV

King Saul did not listen (*shama*). He claimed that *dis*obedience was obedience, but Samuel set him straight. As much as God values our willingness to make sacrifices, he values complete obedience even more.

Our final example to consider is the Israelites, who completely and repeatedly disobeyed God. When they reached the border of the Promised Land, they rebelled and refused to go in.

> And when the LORD sent you out from Kadesh Barnea, he said, "Go up and take possession of the land I have given you." But you rebelled against the command of the LORD your God. You did not trust him or obey [*shama*] him.
>
> Deuteronomy 9:23 NIV

The Israelites heard the words, but they did not trust God and, therefore, did not obey. King Saul heard what God said, but he tried to please both the soldiers and God. Samuel concluded that King Saul had rejected God's word.[66]

---

66. 1 Samuel 15:26

Now contrast King Saul's obedience with Abraham's. Abraham heard what God said and fully obeyed. His obedience was a result of his faith:

> By faith Abraham, when called to go to a place he would later receive as his inheritance, obeyed and went, even though he did not know where he was going.
>
> Hebrews 11:8 NIV

"By faith . . . Abraham obeyed." Abraham followed God's instructions because of his faith. Faith and obedience are connected. We also see this in the men mentioned in Hebrews 11 who listened to God and then obeyed in ways that were courageous.

> And what more shall I say? I do not have time to tell about Gideon, Barak, Samson, Jephthah, David, Samuel and the prophets, who through faith conquered kingdoms, administered justice, and gained what was promised; who shut the mouths of lions, quenched the fury of the flames, and escaped the edge of the sword; whose weakness was turned to strength; and who became powerful in battle and routed foreign armies. Women received back their dead, raised to life again. Others were tortured and refused to be released, so that they might gain a better resurrection. Some faced jeers and flogging, while still others were chained and put in prison. They were stoned; they were sawed in two; they were put to death by the sword. They went about in sheepskins and goatskins, destitute, persecuted and mistreated--the world was not worthy of them. They wandered in deserts and mountains, and in caves and holes in the ground.
>
> Hebrews 11:32-38 NIV

The Hebrew writer singled out these men and women for their faith, but they could also be singled out for their obedience. It was obeying God that put them at odds with the people around them and ultimately got them stoned, sawed in two, persecuted and mistreated. They paid a price to obey. Had they claimed to have faith, but had not obeyed, they likely would not have been persecuted. But that would also mean that they would not have pleased God.

The personal cost of obedience is perhaps the greatest challenge we face today. The world can be cruel to anyone who puts God ahead of everything else. What will other people think if I obey God? Will I look foolish? What price will I pay in the business world or my social life if I hold to God's commands? The choices faced by the men and women of Hebrews 11 were not much different, but they listened to God and obeyed. They were convinced that their relationship with God was worth more than everything they could have in the world.

Our obedience not only confirms our faith in God, it shows that we love him. We go to great lengths to win the love of someone on earth that we care about, so why should loving God be any different? Why would God be satisfied to show us His love and favor if we take His favor to mean that we do not need to obey Him? Anyone who really loves God will obey him:

> We know that we have come to know him <u>if we obey his commands</u>. The man who says, "I know him," but does not do what he commands is a liar, and the truth is not in him. But <u>if anyone obeys his word</u>, God's love is truly made complete in him. This is how we know we are in him: Whoever claims to live in him must walk as Jesus did. [Emphasis added.]
>
> 1 John 2:3-6 NIV

To explain this passage, let's start with an application. Have you ever thought you were in love and wondered how can I be sure? Or how can I know that the person I love really loves me in return? Love is hard to explain; we often settle for the answer, "When you are really in love, you will know." But John says we can know when we really love God. When we know him, we love him and obey him.

What comes first, love or obedience? The answer is that love is both a reason for obeying God and a result of our obedience. The more we do one, the more we will have of the other. And when we overcome obstacles to loving God, his love is made complete.

...If anyone loves me, he <u>will obey [*tereo*] my teaching</u>. My Father will love him, and we will come to him and make our home with him. He who does not love me will not obey [*tereo*] my teaching. [Emphasis added.]

John 14:23-24 NIV

Where the NIV reads "obey my teaching," the NASB reads "keep my word." The Greek word translated "obey" or "keep" is *tereo*.

Definition of *tereo*: 1. to retain in custody, *keep watch over, guard*; 2. to cause a state, condition, or activity to continue, *keep, hold, reserve, preserve*; 3. to persist in obedience, *keep, observe, fulfill, pay attention to.*[67]

Persisting in obedience is an ongoing part of our relationship with God. Our love for God is why we keep listening to what he says and keep obeying him, even when a number of forces are working against us.

In today's world, obedience is wholly underrated. Paul taught a lot about obedience, and even wrote that the purpose of his apostleship was to teach obedience that comes from faith;[68] but what he wrote about being saved by grace gets far more attention than what he wrote about obedience. We like hearing about God's grace, but we won't be saved if we do not obey Him. God's grace does not lessen the need for obedience—if anything, it makes obedience more exciting and rewarding. And God expects us to wholeheartedly obey:

Do you not know that when you present yourselves to someone *as* slaves for obedience, you are slaves of the one whom you obey, either of sin resulting in death, or of obedience resulting in righteousness? But thanks be to God that though you were slaves of sin, you became obedient from the heart to that form of teaching to which you were committed.

Romans 6:16-17 NASB

---

67. <u>BDAG</u>, p.1002.

68. Romans 1:5

Paul encouraged the Christians to wholeheartedly follow the instructions God had given them. In Romans and Galatians, he explained how doing that would require living by faith instead of by the law. By emphasizing faith, he in no way minimized the importance of obedience.

Faith and obedience are critical in our relationship with God. Whether we faithfully obey or not can have far-reaching consequences. We cannot claim to have faith without being obedient to God, nor can we please God by just obeying without faith—neither will compensate for a lack of the other.

Satan wins if we settle for partial obedience or fall for his suggestion that our lack of obedience is justified, given our personal situation. He also wins if we put off obeying because we think we are just not up to the challenge. That is why obedience and faith are connected. It is at those times that we realize how important it is that we obey God and give him a chance to build our faith. Remember that God values obedience even more than the sacrifices we make.

Conversely, sometimes we can think that we are more faithful than we are. This is particularly true if we legalistically hold to a high standard of obedience. Obedience can mask a low standard of faith. We can tend to think of our relationship with God primarily in terms of doing the right thing, instead of in terms of being faithful. That may require some thought to appreciate. We will look at this more in the next chapter.

WORKSHEET 5 – Grace, Faith & Obedience

1. How does being aware of the favor of God in your life help you
    have faith?

    _____

    _____

    _____

    _____

    _____

    _____

    _____

    _____

    _____

    _____

2. How are your faith and your obedience connected?

    _____

    _____

    _____

    _____

    _____

    _____

    _____

    _____

    _____

    _____

    _____

3. What reasons might we have for obeying other than faith?

_____

_____

_____

_____

_____

_____

_____

_____

_____

_____

4. What are the potential long-term effects of obeying for reasons other than faith?

_____

_____

_____

_____

_____

_____

_____

_____

_____

_____

_____

Chapter Notes:

Chapter 6

Grace & the Law

Christians do not live under the Jewish law, so why talk about grace and the law? This subject is important because legalistic righteousness can be as much of a challenge for us today as it was for the Jews. We can, for example, focus more on keeping a list of rules than on doing what pleases God. We can go to church, read our bibles or help the poor because we wrongly assume that those things will save us. Over time, our relationship with God can become routine or, worse yet, a burden instead of a joy. The reasons could be many. We can keep on doing the right things year after year, but forget why we do them. We can mentally check off what we do to assure ourselves that God must be pleased with us. We can drift into doing just enough so as not to feel guilty, or just to satisfy ourselves that we are better than most people.

Misconceptions about grace and the law can cause us to miss what makes our most important relationship so rewarding. In Paul's letters, especially Romans and Galatians, he addressed principles that are the foundation of our relationship with God and how we can be righteous in His eyes. In this chapter, we will focus specifically on what Paul wrote about grace and the law.

Jews and some Jewish Christians misunderstood the purpose of the Jewish law. Even some Gentile Christians were confused about whether or not they should obey it. What Paul wrote about grace and the law can be challenging for us to understand too, but for different reasons. Before we can understand how grace is different from the law, we first have to understand God's purpose in giving the Jews the law, and resolve modern day misconceptions about His grace. Paul's teachings will help us answer the following questions:

- What was the purpose of the Jewish law?

- What did Abraham discover?

- Who is a true child of Abraham?

- What did God accomplish by sending Jesus?

To set the stage, Paul's teachings challenged long-held beliefs of the Jews. The question of who could be a child of God was especially controversial; how was it possible for Gentiles to be saved? Jews looked down upon Gentiles, but in God's eyes, the Jews were no more deserving than the Gentiles. In fact, Jews were judging Gentiles for doing things they were doing themselves.[69] And, to make matters worse, the Jews mistook God's patience in dealing with them for approval of what they were doing.

The Jews had the law and should have known what God expected, but they had not lived up to what they knew. And to add fuel to the fire, Paul declared that people without the law who sought to please God were better off than those with the law who, in reality, cared more about pleasing themselves. In so many words, Paul said, "You law-keepers are not as righteous as you think." They were in desperate need of the gospel, but did not realize it. In fact, by their hypocrisy, they had brought dishonor on God. What brought the issue to a head, though, was what Paul wrote about circumcision:

> If those who are not circumcised keep the law's requirements, will they not be regarded as though they were circumcised? The one who is not circumcised physically and yet obeys the

---

69. Romans 2:1

law will condemn you who, even though you have the written code and circumcision, are a lawbreaker.

A man is not a Jew if he is only one outwardly, nor is circumcision merely outward and physical. No, a man is a Jew if he is one inwardly; and circumcision is circumcision of the heart, by the Spirit, not by the written code. Such a man's praise is not from men, but from God.

What advantage, then, is there in being a Jew, or what value is there in circumcision? Much in every way! First of all, they have been entrusted with the very words of God.

Romans 2:26 - 3:2 NIV

If a Jew broke any part of the law, it would be as though he had not been circumcised. Being circumcised and keeping *most* of the law was no more beneficial than a non-Jew acting like a Jew by being circumcised. Hearing this, a Jew would wonder: "If circumcision doesn't count unless I keep the law perfectly and no one can keep all of the law, and if people who were not circumcised can be treated as though they were, what good is there in being a Jew?" Paul wrote, "Much in every way." Knowing the commands of God was a big advantage.

The same is true for us today. We have easy access to the wisdom of God, and must carefully consider what we do with it. How will we respond when the scriptures challenge what we believe? Jews, who were challenged by what Paul was communicating, came up with some strange reasoning. Paul seemed to mock their excuses:

But if our unrighteousness brings out God's righteousness more clearly, what shall we say? That God is unjust in bringing his wrath on us? (I am using a human argument.) Certainly not! If that were so, how could God judge the world? Someone might argue, "If my falsehood enhances God's truthfulness and so increases his glory, why am I still condemned as a sinner?"

Romans 3:5-7 NIV

Evidently, some Jews reasoned that even if they were sinners, God should not be hard on them because their failure gave God a chance to show his goodness. And besides, letting them fail would reflect poorly on God's faithfulness. But Paul's response to this line of reasoning was abrupt: "Their condemnation is deserved."[70] In other words, that thinking is ridiculous. The failure of men to be faithful to God does not make God unfaithful. God will always be faithful.

A Jew could then wonder, "If the law cannot make me righteous, what was the purpose of the law?"

What was the purpose of the Jewish law?

God gave the Israelites the law soon after they were freed from Egyptian bondage and began their new government. This was the beginning of a new era in the history of the Israelites. They benefited greatly from the wisdom and protection afforded them by the law. Quarantine laws, for example, prevented the spread of disease, and laws regarding food kept them from getting sick. These laws, in particular, were far ahead of the medical knowledge at that time, and having them was a great blessing for the Israelites. The law also guided them in their relationships with each other and with God himself. It covered everything, from what they were permitted to eat to acceptable worship and how to treat other people. The law could be summed up as "Love your neighbor as yourself."[71] God had other purposes for the law that would be clear only after the arrival of Jesus.

The law was good in many ways, but there was a problem. Even the most zealous Jews could not keep it perfectly. In fact, no one could obey enough to be saved. Both Jews and Gentiles were accountable for their sin. Paul summarized the problem and the solution:

> Therefore no one will be declared righteous in his sight by observing the law; rather, through the law we become conscious of sin. But now a righteousness from God, apart from law, has been made known, to which the Law and the Prophets testify. This righteousness from God comes through faith in Jesus Christ to all who believe. There is no difference, for all have sinned and fall short of the glory of God,

---

70. Romans 3:8 NIV

71. Galatians 5:14 NIV

and are justified freely by his grace [*charis*] through the re-demption that came by Christ Jesus. God presented him as a sacrifice of atonement, through faith in his blood. He did this to demonstrate his justice, because in his forbearance he had left the sins committed beforehand unpunished--he did it to demonstrate his justice at the present time, so as to be just and the one who justifies those who have faith in Jesus. [Emphasis added.]

Romans 3:20-26 NIV

We who are Jews by birth and not "Gentile sinners" know that a man is not justified by observing the law, but by faith in Jesus Christ. So we, too, have put our faith in Christ Jesus that we may be justified by faith in Christ and not by observing the law, because by observing the law no one will be justified. [Emphasis added.]

Galatians 2:15-16 NIV

No one will be declared righteous in God's eyes by keeping the Jewish law. The law defined sin, but the Jews were unable to keep it, so they were no better off than the Gentiles. But by God's grace (favor), those who put their faith in the blood of Jesus will be declared innocent of the charges against them. God demonstrated a unique kind of justice. He left the sins committed under the law unpunished, then "at the present time" (after the law), he justifies those who have faith in Jesus. God showed mercy by letting mankind's sins go unpunished until it was time to send Jesus.

The Jews did not deserve to be accepted by God, and God was not obligated to bless them. But "freely by his grace," God gave them a way to be righteous.

Where, then, is boasting? It is excluded. On what principle? On that of observing the law? No, but on that of faith. For we maintain that a man is justified by faith apart from observing the law. Is God the God of Jews only? Is he not the God of Gentiles too? Yes, of Gentiles too, since there is only one

93

> God, who will <u>justify the circumcised by faith and the uncir-</u>
> <u>cumcised through that same faith</u>. [Emphasis added.]
>
> Romans 3:27-30 NIV

> Clearly <u>no one is justified before God by the law</u>, because,
> "The righteous will live by faith." The law is <u>not based on</u>
> <u>faith</u>; on the contrary, "The man who does these things will
> live by them." [Emphasis added.]
>
> Galatians 3:11-12 NIV

Both the circumcised and uncircumcised are justified by faith apart from observing the law. Neither has anything to boast about. Despite Paul's teaching, however, Jews expected God to declare them righteous for obeying the law. They were in for a surprise. Instead of receiving God's approval, those who relied on the law would be condemned. The law was not based on faith, and faithless rule-keeping did not bring anyone closer to God. So what does all this say about the law? What purpose did it serve?

> What, then, was the purpose of the law? It was <u>added because</u>
> <u>of transgressions</u> until the Seed to whom the promise referred
> had come. [Emphasis added.]
>
> Galatians 3:19a NIV

> Before this faith came, we were held prisoners by the law,
> locked up <u>until faith should be revealed</u>. So the law was put
> in charge <u>to lead us to Christ</u> that we might be justified by
> faith. Now that <u>faith has come</u>, we are <u>no longer under the</u>
> <u>supervision of the law</u>. [Emphasis added.]
>
> Galatians 3:23-25 NIV

The law served several purposes. In the most general sense, it was designed to lead the Jews to a relationship with Jesus. The law made it clear that no man had the power to be righteous by keeping a list of rules. The only way they could be saved from the consequences of their sin was by putting their faith in God—and ultimately Jesus. But the Jews had such a difficult time with Jesus that they persuaded the Romans to crucify Him. They also fought long and hard to defend the law and their way of life. And because the Jews felt they were better than Gentiles, they questioned how Gentiles, who had not even tried to keep the law, could be considered worthy by God. To deal with the issues the Jews were facing, Paul posed a thought-provoking question: "What then shall we say that Abraham, our forefather, discovered in this matter?"[72]

What did Abraham discover?

The context of this question concerns Abraham's righteousness and his relationship with God. It is an interesting question because Abraham lived long before there was a Jewish law. Here is some of what we know about Abraham. When he was seventy-five years old, God called him to leave his country and go to a place He would show him.[73] God promised to bless him and make him into a great nation. Abraham obeyed and headed for Canaan.

Think how hard it would be to do something like that today. It is common for people to move to another city for college or to take a new job, but what about moving solely for spiritual reasons? Would your friends think it was a good decision? Thinking about these challenges will help us have a better picture of Abraham's faithfulness to God.

After Abraham arrived in Canaan, there was a severe famine. He took it upon himself to go to Egypt. Eventually, God rescued Abraham and Sarah from the trouble he got into as a result of that decision.[74] Then Abraham returned to Canaan.

Ten years later, despite God's promise to make him into a great nation, Abraham and Sarah still had no children. That's a long time to wait for God to make something happen. Sarah doubted that God would ever bless her with a son, so she urged Abraham to take her servant, Hagar, to be his wife. He did, and when Abraham was eighty-six, Hagar bore a son, Ishmael.

---

72. Romans 4:1 NIV

73. Genesis 12:1-7 (This was before God changed Abram's name to Abraham and his wife Sarai's name to Sarah.)

74. Genesis 12:10-20

When Abraham was ninety-nine, the Lord promised him that he would be the father of kings,[75] and repeated the promise that he and Sarah would have a son. Abraham questioned how a man who was a hundred years old and a woman who was ninety could have a child, and asked God to bless Ishmael instead. God agreed to bless Ishmael, but promised to establish an everlasting covenant with a son born to Sarah. Then, within the year, Sarah gave birth to Isaac, just as God had promised. Note that after God promised to make him into a great nation, Abraham waited twenty-five years for Sarah to have a son.

Sometime later, God tested Abraham's faith by telling him to sacrifice Isaac as a burnt offering.[76] Even though Isaac was the long-awaited son of promise, the very next morning Abraham took Isaac, along with wood for the fire, and headed for the spot the Lord had told him about. On the third day, Abraham saw the place up ahead, and told his servants to wait while he and Isaac went there to worship. Then, Abraham made this remarkable statement: "We will worship and then we will come back to you."[77] Abraham was convinced that both he and Isaac would return after the sacrifice.

When Abraham was about to slay his son, the angel of the Lord stopped him, saying, "Do not lay a hand on the boy. Do not do anything to him. Now I know that you fear God, because you have not withheld from me your son, your only son."[78] Abraham's obedience proved that Abraham had great faith. Then Abraham looked up and saw a ram caught in a thicket, and sacrificed the ram in place of his son.

> <u>By faith</u> Abraham, when God tested him, offered Isaac as a sacrifice. He who had received the promises was about to sacrifice his one and only son, even though God had said to him, "It is through Isaac that your offspring will be reckoned." <u>Abraham reasoned that God could raise the dead</u>, and

---

75. Genesis 17:1-8
76. Genesis 22:1-18
77. Genesis 22:5b NIV
78. Genesis 22:12 NIV

figuratively speaking, he did receive Isaac back from death. [Emphasis added.]

Hebrews 11:17-19 NIV

Only a faithful man would think like Abraham. He counted on God raising Isaac from the dead. So with that in mind, let's examine the intriguing question Paul posed about Abraham:

> What then shall we say that Abraham, our forefather, discovered in this matter? If, in fact, Abraham was justified by works, he had something to boast about--but not before God. What does the Scripture say? "Abraham believed God, and it was credited to him as righteousness." [Emphasis added.]

Romans 4:1-3 NIV

Abraham did many things that could be considered good works. To settle a dispute, he gave his nephew Lot first choice of the land. Later he rescued Lot, who had been taken captive in a war. Then in the interest of honoring God's name, Abraham refused the plunder from the King of Sodom, and gave a tenth of everything he had to Melchizedek, priest of God most high.[79] However, good works were not why Abraham was justified. Abraham had not done anything worthy of boasting before God. His obedience was based on faith, not keeping a law.

> For it is by grace you have been saved, through faith—and this not from yourselves, it is the gift of God—not by works, so that no one can boast.

Ephesians 2:8-9 NIV

Paul also contrasted Abraham's relationship with God to that of a hired hand:

> Now when a man works, his wages are not credited to him as a gift, but as an obligation. However, to the man who does not work but trusts God who justifies the wicked, his faith is credited as righteousness.

Romans 4:4-5 NIV

---

79. Genesis 14:18-24

Abraham's obedience put him in situations where God could bless him, but God was not obligated, like a master who owed a laborer his wages. The application for the Jews was that God was not obligated to bless them for anything they did. The real issue was whether or not they would trust God. Abraham's example was relevant because Abraham was recognized by God for his faith even before there was a Jewish law to obey. In fact, God did not give the Jewish law until over 400 years after His promise to Abraham.

When God had commanded that Abraham and the males in his household be circumcised, Abraham obeyed without hesitation. Certainly God was pleased, but Paul was careful to note that God considered Abraham righteous even *before* he was circumcised.[80] It had nothing to do with the requirement of circumcision in the Jewish law, and everything to do with Abraham's faith and relationship with God. So what was it that Abraham discovered? Was he obeying God because of his faith or because he was keeping a law? If you had asked him that question, Abraham would most likely have answered, "What law?" Abraham was considered righteous long before there was a law. So if Abraham could be righteous by his faith and without keeping a law, the Gentiles could also be considered righteous by their faith.

Think about the difference between the relationship the Jews had with God under the law and the relationship Abraham had with God under the promise.

- *The law* was an agreement to consider a person righteous if they met every condition. But since man could not keep the whole law, no one could be declared righteous.

- *God's promise* to Abraham depended on God's *grace* and Abraham's *faithful* responses to God's commands.

Picture yourself in both situations and consider the difference. Abraham trusted God, and his relationship with God was personal. In contrast, a person whose righteousness depended on keeping the law

---

80. Romans 4:9-12

would not even think in terms of trust. The relationship would be very *im*personal. We see this in the Pharisees who rejected and ultimately crucified Jesus.

Abraham had the kind of personal relationship with God that God wants with each of us. God wanted the same thing before, during and after the law. We also see from Abraham's life, and hopefully from our own lives as well, that nothing is too hard for the lord.

> Without weakening in his faith, he faced the fact that his body was as good as dead--since he was about a hundred years old--and that Sarah's womb was also dead. Yet he did not waver through unbelief regarding the promise of God, but was <u>strengthened in his faith</u> and gave glory to God, <u>being fully persuaded</u> that God had power to do what he had promised. [Emphasis added.]
>
> Romans 4:19-21 NIV

God blessed Abraham's decision to go to a place he had not seen. Later, Abraham and Sarah had a son when the facts would say Sarah's womb was dead. And God responded powerfully when Abraham believed that God would raise Isaac from the dead. Abraham knew that nothing was too hard for the Lord.

How well can you relate to Abraham? Think about what Abraham went through to be faithful to God, and consider how the world we live in would respond to Abraham today. Would people admire Abraham for his faith and convictions or would they think he was crazy? Abraham's faith enabled him to make choices that did not make sense in the eyes of the world, but were pleasing to God.

Even though Abraham became a man of great faith, we can still see the realness in his relationship with God. When God made the promise to make him the father of nations through a son who would be born later, Abraham did not immediately and enthusiastically embrace God's direction. Abraham laughed to himself, then basically asked God to bless the son he already had (born to Hagar), instead of waiting for a son to be born to Sarah. But God reaffirmed his plan, and Abraham went along. Abraham did not know at the time that God had a purpose for making a distinction between the role of the son of the slave woman, Hagar, and the son of the free woman, Sarah.[81]

Abraham was not perfect, but we see God's favor at work in his life. Abraham had his own opinions about what should happen in different situations, but we know him now as a man of great faith because he was willing to let God decide what he should do. By the time God tested Abraham by telling him to sacrifice his son Isaac, Abraham was sure that God would raise Isaac from the dead.

Abraham obeyed many times without knowing all the details of how things would work out. His relationship with God came before his need to know all the results, and he was patient when things did not happen quickly. For example, Abraham waited twenty-five years for Isaac to be born. We should remember this when we don't quickly get what we think God should give us. Our relationship with God is more important than any blessings we think we need.

Abraham lived by faith. Let's consider more in-depth what that means:

> And without faith it is impossible to please God, because anyone who comes to him must believe that he exists and that he rewards those who earnestly seek him.
>
> Hebrews 11:6 NIV

There are two aspects to the faith described here. First, we must believe that God exists, and second, we must believe that God will reward us if we put him first in our lives. We know that Abraham had *faith in God*, but it will give us a clearer picture of what that means if we say that Abraham had *faith in God's favor*. In other words, Abraham had faith that God would reward him (show him favor) for trusting Him to provide what he needed and obeying his commands.

This is something we all need to contemplate in our own relationship with God: Do I believe God exists? Do I believe He will reward

---

81. Galatians 4:21-31

me if I earnestly seek Him? Do I trust His goodness? Have you ever thought to yourself or even voiced the concern that, "I don't know if I can trust God?" Not trusting God's goodness gives Satan an opportunity to work against us. If you struggle with trusting God or with letting Him have control of your life, you have room to grow in your understanding of God's favor and goodness. Abraham let God direct and sometimes redirect his life.

As I conclude this discussion of what Abraham discovered, I want you to think about what you might discover in your relationship with God. Are you willing to do whatever God calls you to do? If not, what needs to change? When you think about the challenges you face in your life today, are you certain that nothing is too hard for the Lord? Do you focus more on building your relationship with God or on how to achieve specific results? Are you happy to let God decide what those results are?

There is more to what Abraham did than just having faith. You have probably heard people say, "All you have to do is believe." I guess you could say all Abraham had to do when God told him to sacrifice Isaac was believe, but that would be a huge understatement. If you were Abraham, would you look back on the challenges in your life and say, "All I ever had to do to was believe?" It is not enough to say, "I have faith," you must act on your faith. Abraham's obedience showed that he had faith. James, the brother of Jesus, must have been thinking that when he wrote this about Abraham:

> Was not our ancestor Abraham considered righteous for what he did when he offered his son Isaac on the altar? You see that his faith and his actions were working together, and his faith was made complete by what he did. And the scripture was fulfilled that says, "Abraham believed God, and it was credited to him as righteousness," and he was called God's friend. You see that a person is justified by what he does and not by faith alone.

> In the same way, was not even Rahab the prostitute considered righteous for what she did when she gave lodging to the spies and sent them off in a different direction? As the body without the spirit is dead, so faith without deeds is dead.
>
> James 2:21-26 NIV

In this passage, James cites Genesis 15:6, just as Paul did in Romans 4:3. Paul used the same passage to show that Abraham was not justified simply because he did enough to deserve it, but because of his faith. James explains that if Abraham claimed to have faith, but had not obeyed, he would have come to a dead end. Both statements are true. If they were not, we would not read about Abraham's faith in Hebrews 11. But because Abraham was willing to sacrifice Isaac, as God commanded, the angel of the Lord said, "Now I know that you fear God."[82]

If Abraham had waited to obey until he had more faith, he might never have obeyed. But Abraham understood what it meant to have God's favor, and obeying God was the only reasonable response. For Abraham, it was not about the results, but about his relationship with God.

Who is a true son of Abraham?

Remember that our purpose for asking this and the other three questions posed in the beginning of this chapter is to understand and apply what Paul wrote about grace and the law. The significance of this particular question is that only children of Abraham are heirs of the promise. God's promise to Abraham included his descendants:

> I will establish my covenant as an everlasting covenant between me and you and <u>your descendants after you for the generations to come</u>, to be your God and the God of your descendants after you. [Emphasis added.]
>
> Genesis 17:7 NIV

---

82. Genesis 22:12

The Jews were descendants of Abraham by birth and God's chosen people,[83] so they naturally assumed they were heirs to the promise. But beginning with John the Baptist, that assumption was called into question.

> Produce fruit in keeping with repentance. And do not think you can say to yourselves, "We have Abraham as our father." I tell you that out of these stones God can raise up children for Abraham.
>
> Matthew 3:8-9 NIV

Jesus also made an issue of who was a child of Abraham. When Jesus told the Pharisees that those who held to his teaching would be "set free," they responded: "We are Abraham's descendants and have never been slaves of anyone. How can you say that we shall be set free?"[84] They were thinking of slavery in the physical sense, not in a spiritual way, and they were quick to point out that Abraham was their father. "If you were Abraham's children," said Jesus, "then you would do the things Abraham did."[85] What Jesus meant was probably not as obvious to the Jews who listened to him then as it is to us reading about it now.

Paul dealt with this issue repeatedly with both the Jews and the Gentiles. He taught that people who were not physical descendants of Abraham could be his spiritual children by their faith:

> It was not through law that Abraham and his offspring received the promise that he would be heir of the world, but through the righteousness that comes by faith. For if those who live by law are heirs, faith has no value and the promise is worthless, because law brings wrath. And where there is no law there is no transgression.
>
> Therefore, the promise comes by faith, so that it may be by grace and may be guaranteed to all Abraham's offspring--not only to those who are of the law but also to those who are of

---

83. Deuteronomy 7:6

84. John 8:33 NIV

85. John 8:39b NIV

the faith of Abraham. He is the father of us all. As it is written: "I have made you a father of many nations." He is our father in the sight of God, in whom he believed--the God who gives life to the dead and calls things that are not as though they were. [Emphasis added.]

Romans 4:13-17 NIV

Understand, then, that those who believe are children of Abraham.

Galatians 3:7 NIV

True sons of Abraham were (and are) those who have the faith of Abraham. God opened the door to the Gentiles who could be heirs of His promise to Abraham, even though they were not Abraham's physical descendants and had not kept the law. They could become his children by their faith.

This was great news for the Gentiles, but it was very challenging for the Jews. Being a child of Abraham meant everything to the Jews. They relied heavily on their status as the chosen ones, so even suggesting that they were not the children of the promise was questioning the whole of their religion. Jews would wonder how could this be?

It is not as though God's word had failed. For not all who are descended from Israel are Israel. Nor because they are his descendants are they all Abraham's children. On the contrary, "It is through Isaac that your offspring will be reckoned." In other words, it is not the natural children who are God's children, but it is the children of the promise who are regarded as Abraham's offspring. [Emphasis added.]

Romans 9:6-8 NIV

There was nothing wrong with God's word; the issue was something else. To explain further, Paul cites two precedents that Jews would be able to understand. First, both Ishmael and Isaac were sons of Abraham, Isaac by Sarah and Ishmael by Hagar; however, the Jews did not consider Ishmael's descendants (the Arabs) to be "chosen." Similarly, Esau and Jacob were twin sons of Isaac and Rebekah, but the Jews did not count Esau's descendants (the Edomites) among the chosen.[86] So the Jews showed by their own actions that Abraham's descendants were not all treated the same.

The Jews knew what Paul was talking about, but did not like his conclusions. You and I have a different challenge. Paul's writing can be confusing for us because we are not as well-versed in Jewish history. Consider Paul's explanation:

> For this was how the promise was stated: "At the appointed time I will return, and Sarah will have a son."
>
> Not only that, but Rebekah's children had one and the same father, our father Isaac. Yet, underline before the twins were born or had done anything good or bad--in order that God's purpose in election might stand: not by works but by him who calls-- she was told, "The older will serve the younger." Just as it is written: "Jacob I loved, but Esau I hated."
>
> What then shall we say? Is God unjust? Not at all! For he says to Moses, "I will have mercy on whom I have mercy, and I will have compassion on whom I have compassion." It does not, therefore, depend on man's desire or effort, but on God's mercy. [Emphasis added.]
>
> Romans 9:9-16 NIV

This was not a lesson on fairness; it was about the sovereignty of God. God has the last word on who receives his mercy (compassion). By choosing to bless one son and not the other, before either had done anything to influence his decision, God showed that his mercy is given and not earned. God does not owe us anything, no matter how obedient we are. And God is in no way obligated to treat us in a way we think is fair.

Both Ishmael and Isaac were sons of Abraham, but God told Abraham to reject Ishmael[87] because Isaac was the son of promise. Similarly, before twins were born to Isaac and Rebekah, God told

---

86. W. Barclay, Barclay's Daily Study Bible (NT), WORD*search* 8.0.2.40 (WORD*search* Corp, 2008).

87. Genesis 21:12; Romans 9:7-8

Rebekah that the older would serve the younger.[88] God's choose the line of Jacob over the line of Esau. It was His will. Therefore, Jacob, who received the promise, could not argue that he deserved it any more than Esau. God will show mercy to whomever he wants to show mercy. So the Jews were no more entitled to be considered righteous than the Gentiles. And God could have mercy on the Gentiles if he wanted to have mercy on them.

Paul used Abraham as an example to make a similar point to the Galatians.

> Consider Abraham: "He believed God, and it was credited to him as righteousness." Understand, then, that <u>those who believe are children of Abraham</u>. The Scripture foresaw that God would justify the Gentiles by faith, and <u>announced the gospel in advance to Abraham: "All nations will be blessed through you.</u>" So those who have faith are blessed along with Abraham, the man of faith. [Emphasis added.]
>
> Galatians 3:6-9 NIV

So the true sons of Abraham are those who have the faith of Abraham, not those who were his descendants by birth. And the Gentiles could be sons of Abraham and heirs to the promise, even though they were not his descendants and did not keep the law. They became his children by their faith.

This was incredibly good news. But even among the Gentiles there was some confusion about the law. Did they now need to start keeping the law? Even some Jewish Christians felt that Paul had wrongly relaxed the ceremonial requirements of the law for the benefit of the Gentiles. They tried to convince Gentile Christians to obey at least portions of the law, and some Gentiles were misled by their teaching.

The situation was serious, so Paul rebuked them: "Are you so foolish? After beginning with the Spirit, are you now trying to attain your goal by human effort?"[89] Keeping rules does not mean you have a rela-

---

88. Genesis 25:23
89. Galatians 3:3 NIV

tionship with God, and rule-keeping would not make the Gentiles any more righteous than it did the Jews:

> Mark my words! I, Paul, tell you that if you let yourselves be circumcised, Christ will be of no value to you at all. Again I declare to every man who lets himself be circumcised that he is obligated to obey the whole law. You who are trying to be justified by law have been alienated from Christ; you have fallen away from grace. [Emphasis added.]
>
> Galatians 5:2-4 NIV

If the Gentile Christians let themselves be circumcised, it would be as if Jesus had not died for their sins, and they would be obligated to obey all of the Jewish law. Giving up the favor of God to live under the Jewish law was "falling away from grace"—or falling out of favor with God. They would essentially be saying, "I can do this without God."

The Jews were dealing with much the same issue, only instead of falling from grace, they were refusing the offer to rely on it. They preferred to rely on the law to save them. Instead of welcoming the end of a law—a law they could not fully obey—they did all they could to hold on to it and put a stop to Jesus.

God's expectation that his children would trust him completely and put their faith in Jesus was not unfair to the Jews or too much to expect. If the Jews had realized what God was offering them, and had been willing to humble themselves, the decision would have been easy and the outcome extremely rewarding. (Many Jews did become Christians.) God rewards those who earnestly seek him. We must remember that and be grateful that we do not live under the law.

So, there was nothing wrong with God's promise to bless all nations through Abraham's descendants. God is sovereign and he has the final word on who receives his mercy, and he decided that it would be Abraham's descendants by faith instead of by birth. The true children of Abraham were (and are) the ones with the faith of Abraham.

What did God accomplish by sending Jesus?

What would you think if you opened your morning paper and saw the headline: Wrath of God Revealed in (your city)? Likely, you would read the article quickly to see if you might be affected. We won't know in advance when it will be, but God will deal with man's godless and wicked behavior.[90]

In the beginning of Romans, Paul gave a sobering account of the seriousness of man's sin. He described ungodly people as senseless, faithless, heartless and ruthless, and he made it clear that God would hold them accountable. He then confronted his Jewish brothers by saying that they too were among those in desperate need of a savior. They had long depended on a law that could not save them. But now they could be righteous by putting their faith in Jesus:

> But now a righteousness from God, apart from law, has been made known, to which the Law and the Prophets testify. This righteousness from God <u>comes through faith in Jesus Christ</u> to <u>all who believe</u>. There is no difference, for <u>all have sinned</u> and fall short of the glory of God, and are justified freely <u>by his grace through the redemption that came by Christ Jesus</u>. [Emphasis added.]
>
> Romans 3:21-24 NIV

Instead of punishing men for their sins, God sent his son Jesus to die so that those who put their faith in him could be forgiven. "By his grace" describes God's motivation for paying such a high price for redeeming us; the life of Jesus was what it cost. And everyone has sinned, so no one could say they did not need Jesus. But even though the Jewish law and the Prophets testified that one day a Messiah would come, the Jews largely refused to accept that Jesus was that Messiah.

Paul had an interesting vantage point as to what the Jews were facing. He was known as an expert in the law, but now realized that he had devoted much of his life to keeping a law that could not save him. He saw how unworthy he was to have God's favor. Paul declared, "What a

---

90. Romans 1:18-20

wretched man I am."[91] That's why he was so grateful to God, and why he wanted his Jewish brothers to have what he had in Jesus.

Compare Paul's response to that of the Jews. Even though they had the benefit of the law and had heard the prophecies about the Messiah, they hardened their hearts to Jesus' message and refused to follow him. They claimed to follow God, but would not follow his Son. So what happened?

> What then shall we say? That the Gentiles, who did not pursue righteousness, have obtained it, a righteousness that is by faith; but Israel, who pursued a law of righteousness, has not attained it. Why not? Because they pursued it not by faith but as if it were by works. They stumbled over the "stumbling stone." As it is written: "See, I lay in Zion a stone that causes men to stumble and a rock that makes them fall, and the one who trusts in him will never be put to shame."
>
> Romans 9:30-33 NIV

Paul quoted Isaiah 8:14 and 28:16, two scriptures that early Christians associated with Jesus. The "stone that causes men to stumble" was Jesus. They stumbled because their traditions were more important to them than living by faith.[92] Their hearts were so calloused by their legalistic religion they could not hear anything different, or understand and change their course.[93]

Here we see how deeply concerned Paul was for the Jews:

> Brothers, my heart's desire and prayer to God for the Israelites is that they may be saved. For I can testify about them that they are zealous for God, but their zeal is not based on knowledge. Since they <u>did not know the righteousness that comes from God and sought to establish their own</u>, they did not submit to God's righteousness. <u>Christ is the end of the law</u> so that there may be righteousness for everyone who believes. [Emphasis added.]
>
> Romans 10:1-4 NIV

---

91. Romans 7:24 NIV

92. Mark 7:6-8

93. Acts 28:27

From his own experience, Paul understood what the Jews were up against, but he was also keenly aware of the dangers of not knowing true righteousness from God. He kept reminding Jewish Christians and trying to persuade Jews that Jesus was the end of the law. Then Paul wrapped up his plea by saying that Jesus was their only hope of salvation, and that the Gentiles were included in the promise too:

> "The word is near you; it is in your mouth and in your heart," that is, the word of faith we are proclaiming: That if you confess with your mouth, "<u>Jesus is Lord</u>," and believe in your heart that God raised him from the dead, you will be saved. For it is with your heart that you believe and are justified, and it is with your mouth that you confess and are saved. As the Scripture says, "Anyone who trusts in him will never be put to shame." For there is no difference between Jew and Gentile--the same Lord is Lord of all and richly blesses all who call on him, for, "<u>Everyone who calls on the name of the Lord will be saved</u>." [Emphasis added.]
>
> Romans 10:8-13 NIV

To confess "Jesus is Lord," a Jew had to put everything on the line. It would mean a dramatic change in every part of his life. Paul knew that, but if they did not accept Jesus, they would be lost, because the law did not have the power to save them. So Paul pleaded with the Jews to be saved by calling on the name of Jesus.

Paul's teaching that "Everyone who calls on the name of the Lord will be saved" has been misinterpreted. The emphasis here is not on *how* to be saved, but on *who* saves you. Paul was simply explaining that Jesus was the Lord.

The Jews had a difficult time accepting Jesus, but they understood what it meant to call on someone's name or to claim someone as their Lord. Lordship is more difficult for us to understand, however, because lordship is not part of our culture. To say, "Jesus is Lord" and call on his name is the same as saying that we voluntarily put ourselves under Jesus' Lordship and Sovereignty. We entrust ourselves to him completely and will obey him as our Lord and Master. It is much more than saying the words "Jesus is Lord." We are pledging to obey Him, and live our lives to please Jesus.

Jesus is our Sovereign Lord, who has total authority over our lives, even to the point of deciding life and death. Many people want a savior, but are not interested in having a lord and master. But to follow Jesus, he must be both. Paul understood that and called on Jesus' name when he was baptized. Here is his account of what Ananias told him in Damascus:

> And now what are you waiting for? Get up, be baptized and wash your sins away, <u>calling on his name</u>. [Emphasis added.]
>
> Acts 22:16 NIV

Those who put their faith in Jesus became known as the ones who called on the name of Jesus:

> And he has come here with authority from the chief priests to arrest all who <u>call on your name</u>. [Emphasis added.]
>
> Acts 9:14 NIV

> All those who heard him were astonished and asked, "Isn't he the man who raised havoc in Jerusalem among those <u>who call on this name</u>? And hasn't he come here to take them as prisoners to the chief priests?" [Emphasis added.]
>
> Acts 9:21 NIV

> To the church of God in Corinth, to those sanctified in Christ Jesus and called to be holy, together with all those everywhere who <u>call on the name of our Lord Jesus Christ</u>--their Lord and ours…. [Emphasis added.]
>
> 1 Corinthians 1:2 NIV

Today, if you belong to Christ, you are a child of Abraham and an heir to the promise. Those who are baptized into Christ become children of God through their faith in Jesus.

> Therefore, since we have been justified through faith, we have peace with God through our Lord Jesus Christ, through

> whom we have <u>gained access by faith into this grace</u> in which we now stand. And we rejoice in the hope of the glory of God. [Emphasis added.]
>
> Romans 5:1-2 NIV

Paul described how Christians "gained access by faith into this grace." What an incredible blessing that is. Jesus did for us what we could not do, that is, be good enough to be declared righteous. Jesus was the fullness of God's favor, or as the Apostle John wrote, "grace upon grace."[94] Through Jesus, God would carry out the greatest rescue mission of all time.

> You see, at just the right time, when we were still powerless, Christ died for the ungodly. Very rarely will anyone die for a righteous man, though for a good man someone might possibly dare to die. But God demonstrates his own love for us in this: While we were still sinners, Christ died for us.
>
> Since we have now been justified by his blood, how much more shall we be saved from God's wrath through him! For if, when we were God's enemies, we were reconciled to him through the death of his Son, how much more, having been reconciled, shall we be saved through his life!
>
> Romans 5:6-10 NIV

The mission God accomplished by sending Jesus was to save us from eternal punishment. It began even before Abraham received the promise, and long before the Jews received the law. The law did serve a purpose, but only until the Seed (Jesus) referred to in the promise arrived.[95] Jesus Christ was the end of the law.[96] So the inheritance does not depend on the law, but on the promise God made to Abraham by His grace. And now we too are heirs to the promise through our faith in Jesus Christ.[97] Through Jesus, God accomplished his mission!

---

94. John 1:16 NASB

95. Galatians 3:16-19

96. Romans 10:4

97. Galatians 3:14 NIV

Summary:

What Paul wrote about grace and the law is still relevant to us today. Just like the Jews and Gentiles in Paul's day, we too can make the mistake of relying on things that cannot save us—rule-keeping, traditions, or good works. Two thousand years of Christianity have left us with a lot of religious traditions and rules that people follow which are not based on the Bible. Jesus spoke about the dangers of following traditions:

> He replied, "Isaiah was right when he prophesied about you hypocrites; as it is written: 'These people honor me with their lips, but their hearts are far from me. They worship me in vain; their teachings are but rules taught by men.' You have let go of the commands of God and are holding on to the traditions of men."
>
> And he said to them: "You have a fine way of setting aside the commands of God in order to observe your own traditions!"
>
> Mark 7:6-9 NIV

Jesus denounced men who ignored God's commands and decided for themselves how they would worship Him. Following religious traditions with good intentions, but without knowing God's commands, is vain worship too. It is important that we rely on the scriptures to know what God expects and then obey. Otherwise, we will end up like the Jews who found out that their worship of God was in vain. They did not have a right relationship with God.

Another problem today that has to do with grace and the law is the popular teaching that God's grace alone is what saves you. This teaching disregards the need to obey scriptures that affect one's salvation, such as those that teach the necessity of baptism. Paul reminded the Colossians that they had been buried with Jesus in baptism and raised with him *through their faith* in the power of God.[98] Baptism is an act of faith.

---

98.   Colossians 2:12

What Paul taught about grace should be considered in light of his other teachings about obedience. The reason Paul emphasized grace was to help his readers understand and be thankful for the gift of God's favor, not to say that obedience was unnecessary.

It is by God's grace (favor) that we can be baptized for the forgiveness of our sins and live a purpose-filled life. We cannot, however, simply assume that because we have been baptized, we are righteous before God, any more than the Jews could rely on the fact that they had been circumcised. Baptism without faithfully relying on God will not save us. Like Abraham, we will be saved because of God's favor and our faithful obedience to Him in everything.

WORKSHEET 6 – Grace & the Law

1. What can cause us to drift into a legalistic relationship with God?

_____

_____

_____

_____

_____

_____

_____

_____

_____

_____

_____

_____

2. What are the benefits of living under grace verses the law?

_____

_____

_____

_____

_____

_____

_____

_____

_____

_____

3. How does understanding the favor of God help you keep your relationship with Him from becoming routine?

_____

_____

_____

_____

_____

_____

_____

_____

_____

_____

4. What is the difference between believing that God exists and believing that he rewards those who diligently seek him?

_____

_____

_____

_____

_____

_____

_____

_____

_____

_____

Chapter Notes:

Chapter 7

The Throne of Grace

In the last chapter, we saw the danger of putting our confidence in our own strength and our performance. In this chapter, we will focus on how we can be confident in the favor of God—even when we feel inadequate.

> Let us then approach the throne of grace with confidence, so that we may receive mercy and find grace to help us in our time of need.
>
> Hebrews 4:16 NIV

This verse gives us valuable insight into how personalized God's grace can be. When we realize how much we need God, we can approach Him with confidence and expect to receive His favor and compassion. Typically, though, when we are struggling spiritually, we lack confidence and tend to pull back. And the more inadequate we feel, the less confident we are. But, the writer of Hebrews tells us that we need to think differently. Instead of trying to find the confidence we need somewhere within ourselves, we can look to our loving, compassionate and gracious God. He tells us why we can approach God with confidence:

> For the word of God is living and active. Sharper than any double-edged sword, it penetrates even to dividing soul and

spirit, joints and marrow; it judges the thoughts and attitudes of the heart. Nothing in all creation is hidden from God's sight. Everything is uncovered and laid bare before the eyes of him to whom we must give account.

Therefore, since we have a great high priest who has gone through the heavens, Jesus the Son of God, let us hold firmly to the faith we profess. For we do not have a high priest who is unable to sympathize with our weaknesses, but we have one who has been tempted in every way, just as we are--yet was without sin. <u>Let us then approach the throne of grace with confidence, so that we may receive mercy and find grace to help us in our time of need</u>. [Emphasis added.]

Hebrews 4:12-16 NIV

There are several important lessons in this passage. First, God's word is relevant; it is the standard for knowing if our feelings and thoughts are right or wrong. God's word is the one place we can go to find out if our hearts are in the right place.

Second, we learn that God sees everything. That's scary because we think and do things we know are evil. Most of us try to maintain our image and control what we let the people around us see—we don't want them to know the real us. But we cannot hide anything from God. Think about your week. Did anything happen that you don't want to be held accountable for? Were you deceitful to avoid painful consequences? Did you have an ungodly attitude toward a co-worker or maybe another driver? God watched it all. God not only sees, He heard what you said in your heart. We are even accountable for our attitudes.

You may be asking, "So how will this help me be confident?" The fact that God knows us inside and out, but still loves us and wants a relationship with us helps give us confidence. He did not choose us because we were such good people. He knows every one of our shortcomings. In addition, Jesus is our "great high priest." He knows exactly how we feel and sympathizes with our weaknesses. He has been through similar battles Himself. And later in Hebrews, we read that, as our high priest, Jesus offered himself as a perfect sacrifice on our behalf,[99] and that he appears before God to speak for us.[100] Since we are "laid bare" before God, we are blessed to have Jesus to represent us.

Finally, the passage ends with the verse we began with: "Let us then approach the throne of grace with confidence, so that we may receive mercy and find grace to help us in our time of need." When we need God's favor to help us, and the relief only he can provide, we can confidentially approach him and expect to receive his favor and compassion. What an amazing opportunity! Jesus illustrates this kind of confidence in the parable of the lost son:

> Jesus continued: "There was a man who had two sons. The younger one said to his father, 'Father, give me my share of the estate.' So he divided his property between them. "Not long after that, the younger son got together all he had, set off for a distant country and there squandered his wealth in wild living. After he had spent everything, there was a severe famine in that whole country, and he began to be in need. So he went and hired himself out to a citizen of that country, who sent him to his fields to feed pigs. He longed to fill his stomach with the pods that the pigs were eating, but no one gave him anything.
>
> "When he came to his senses, he said, 'How many of my father's hired men have food to spare, and here I am starving to death! I will set out and go back to my father and say to him: Father, I have sinned against heaven and against you. I am no longer worthy to be called your son; make me like one of your hired men.'"
>
> Luke 15:11-19 NIV

The younger son went off to seek the favor of the world and ended up poor and hungry. When he came to his senses, he realized what he had given up when he left home. He remembered the favor his father had shown him, and wondered if his father would take him

---

99. Hebrews 10:12-14

100. Hebrews 9:24

back. He was even willing to be treated like a servant. (That would take humility.)

> "So he got up and went to his father. But while he <u>was still a long way off</u>, his father saw him and was <u>filled with compassion</u> for him; he <u>ran to his son</u>, threw his arms around him and kissed him.
>
> "The son said to him, 'Father, I have sinned against heaven and against you. <u>I am no longer worthy to be called your son.</u>'" [Emphasis added.]
>
> Luke 15:20-21 NIV

We are not told, but we would understand if the son had second thoughts as he approached the house: "I wasted everything he gave me. Will I be welcome? Will he even let me be one of his servants?"

The father's response would surprise most people. He did not wait to see if his son made it all the way to the house. He also did not withhold his approval to teach him a lesson. Remember that our description for mercy is "the compassion to offer relief." The father showed great compassion. He had been longing for his lost son to return and could not contain his joy. He did everything he could to comfort his son.

> "But the father said to his servants, 'Quick! Bring the best robe and put it on him. Put a ring on his finger and sandals on his feet. Bring the fattened calf and kill it. Let's have a feast and celebrate. For this son of mine was dead and is alive again; he was lost and is found.' So they began to celebrate."
>
> Luke 15:22-24 NIV

"Let's have a feast and celebrate," was how the father responded. Nothing was held back. Even though the son brought his problems on himself, he received compassion and was shown favor by his father. The son said, "I am no longer worthy to be called your son," and, in so many words, the father said, "Yes you are!" The son said, "Make me like one of your hired men,"[101] but the father said, "My son who was dead is alive." So they began to celebrate.

---

101. Luke 15:19 NIV

The younger son's confidence in his father was justified. He received even more than he asked. His father took care of his physical needs with food and clothing, and his spiritual needs by letting him leave the sins of his wild living behind. His father showed him his favor by restoring him to his place as a son.

Jesus told this story to help the Pharisees understand that our Heavenly Father is gracious and compassionate to sinners. This story gives us insight into the favor of God. He is watching for us like the father was watching for his son and responds even when we feel like we are a long way off. Our confidence must be in God and his favor and compassion, not in ourselves.

The younger son's choices were clear: starve or go back to his father. The older son's problem was less obvious, but the consequences of his behavior were equally serious.

> "Meanwhile, the <u>older son</u> was in the field. When he came near the house, he heard music and dancing. So he called one of the servants and asked him what was going on. 'Your brother has come,' he replied, 'and your father has killed the fattened calf because he has him back safe and sound.'
>
> "The older brother <u>became angry and refused to go in</u>. So his father went out and pleaded with him. But he answered his father, 'Look! <u>All these years I've been slaving for you and never disobeyed your orders</u>. Yet you never gave me even a young goat so I could celebrate with my friends. But when this son of yours who has squandered your property with prostitutes comes home, you kill the fattened calf for him!'" [Emphasis added.]

> Luke 15:25-30 NIV

The older son refused to even greet his brother. He called him "this son of yours" in the emotional exchange of words with his father. He was not happy that his brother came home, and perhaps more upset that his father took him back and showed him such favor and compassion. The situation brought out the older son's attitudes: "All these years I have been slaving for you," and "I have never disobeyed your orders." On the outside, he looked like a devoted son, but inside he felt more like a servant. And he viewed his father's helpful instructions as orders. Bitter attitudes hurt his relationship with his father and may have put an end to his relationship with his brother.

It is interesting how two brothers, who grew up in the same house could have vastly different perspectives of their father. The younger son saw his father's compassion and favor. The older son felt like he was his father's servant. Consider this illustration of the difference between a son and a servant:

A servant thinks:
- I am accepted for what I do.
- I am valued because of my workmanship.
- I am only secure if I produce.
- At the end of the day, I'll have some peace if I have proved myself.
- Tomorrow I have to prove myself again.
- If I fail, I could lose my job.

A son thinks:
- I'm accepted for who I am.
- My value comes from my relationship with my father.
- I am secure because my father loves me.
- Success or failure won't change my status.
- Even if I fail, I will still be my father's son.

The older son gives us a picture of what it looks like to live as though pleasing God is our duty. He approached his relationship with his father with the mind-set of a servant instead of a son. What little confidence he had was based on his performance. That prevented him from being able to celebrate. He had his father's favor all along, but missed out on the joy of that relationship. What did he think when his brother left with his share of the inheritance? Was he living for the day when everything else would be his? Did he resent his brother more for wasting his share of his father's estate on wild living, or for coming back and interfering with what should be his? When his younger brother was shown mercy, his attitudes became apparent. The real issue seemed to be the lack of joy in his life. His father tried to help him change his perspective.

> "My son," the father said, "you are always with me, and everything I have is yours. But we had to celebrate and be glad, because this brother of yours was dead and is alive again; he was lost and is found."
>
> Luke 15:31-32 NIV

Jesus did not go on with the story, so we can only imagine what might have happened. But we would do well to consider how we might be like either son, and how the story might end with us. What perspective do we have of God?

The older son lived a life of duty. Day after day he obeyed, but he never enjoyed his place as a son or felt the joy of his father's favor. He had very little in his life to celebrate. However, he had no one to blame but himself. The attitudes and resentments in his heart were what caused him to act more like a servant than a son.

The writer of Hebrews described how things in our heart can cause us to miss out on the favor of God.

> See to it that no one misses the grace of God and that no bitter root grows up to cause trouble and defile many.
>
> Hebrews 12:15 NIV

The older son missed the grace (favor) that could have been his, and became bitter toward his father and his brother. In his pride, he did not take responsibility, but instead blamed his father (and brother) for his unhappiness. However, if he had been humble and gone to his father to help get the things in his heart resolved, he would have had something to celebrate.

The younger son came to realize how much he needed his father's favor, and humbly returned home admitting his sin. This gives us a picture of what it means to draw near to the throne of grace. He approached his father with humility. That is how we should approach God. The fact that God knows everything about us should humble us and allow us to put aside our pretenses and draw close to Him. God may not answer our prayers with a "yes," but we can confidently expect to receive His favor and compassion.

To summarize, God's word invites us to approach God at any time for His favor and compassion. And it explains why we can approach Him with confidence, even when we feel anxious or discouraged: Jesus is the one speaking to God on our behalf, and God is the one who sent Jesus to die for us! We know that God is full of compassion and favor, so let us draw near to him with confidence—confidence in Him, not ourselves.

WORKSHEET 7 – The Throne of Grace

1. When do you feel the greatest need for grace?

2. What might keep you from approaching the throne of grace with confidence?

3. Do you relate more with the younger or older son? Why?

4. What will help you draw near to God when you have thoughts about pulling back?

_____

_____

_____

_____

_____

_____

_____

_____

_____

_____

_____

5. What have you learned about God's grace that will help you never give up your relationship with God?

_____

_____

_____

_____

_____

_____

_____

_____

_____

Chapter Notes:

Chapter 8

Grace Teaches us to Say "No"

For the grace of God that brings salvation has appeared to all men. It teaches us to say "No" to ungodliness and worldly passions, and to live self-controlled, upright and godly lives in this present age, while we wait for the blessed hope--the glorious appearing of our great God and Savior, Jesus Christ, who gave himself for us to redeem us from all wickedness and to purify for himself a people that are his very own, eager to do what is good.

Titus 2:11-14 NIV

We desperately need God's help to say "no" to sin because we live in a world that promotes ungodly behavior in more and different ways every day. Movies, television and the internet promote worldly pleasures and make ungodliness look irresistible. Video games let people "play" with dangerous behavior in a virtual life, supposedly without any consequences. And high tech portable devices let us take the world's influence and whatever captures our attention along with us wherever we go. Then, if our choices lead to undesirable consequences, Satan tells us to blame somebody else.

New gadgets can make our lives easier, but some also make it easier to sin. Labor-saving conveniences are nice, but we have to fight Satan the old-fashioned way, by saying "no" to ungodliness when our sinful nature wants to say "yes." There are no high-tech or even low-tech shortcuts. (However, in many cases, the off button is a powerful and effective weapon against sin.)

To begin with, it is encouraging to know that we *can* say no to sin, even though we have said yes in the past. Still, Satan will not let us escape his snare without a fight. He will do whatever he can to make saying no look unnecessary, if not impossible. He uses half-truths and all kinds of deception. According to Jesus, Satan is a liar and the father of lies.[102] And no one is immune. Satan deceived Eve, who had the ideal life ahead of her, and he has been deceiving people ever since:

> The god of this age has blinded the minds of unbelievers, so that they cannot see the light of the gospel of the glory of Christ, who is the image of God.
>
> 2 Corinthians 4:4 NIV

Spiritual blindness has such a damaging effect on people's lives. The message "Sin and worldly living is fun—don't miss out!" comes at us from every direction, and more people are fooled by it every day. It may not be obvious, and may happen gradually, but it will eventually destroy us. Paul reminded the Christians in Ephesus about the destructiveness of sin:

> You were taught, with regard to your former way of life, to put off your old self, which is being corrupted [*phtheiro*] by its deceitful desires;
>
> Ephesians 4:22 NIV

The Greek word translated "corrupted" in this verse is *phtheiro.*

Definition of *phtheiro*: 1. to cause harm to in a physical manner or in outward circumstances, *destroy, ruin, corrupt, spoil*; 2. to cause deterioration of the inner life, *ruin, corrupt*;

---

102. John 8:44

132

3. to inflict punishment, *destroy*; 4. break rules of a contest, *violate rules.*[103]

Once something becomes corrupted, it is no longer useful for its intended purpose. In common uses of the word *phtheiro*, the harm was caused by immorality or when someone was led astray by erroneous teaching or misleading tactics. In Ephesians 4:22, the deterioration was self-inflicted by giving in to the sinful nature. Jesus told his disciples a parable that illustrates how this can happen. A farmer sowed his seed in his field and some fell on the ground among thorns. When the plants began to grow, the thorns crowded out the good plants and the crop was ruined. When Jesus explained the meaning of the parable to his disciples, we learn what he meant by thorns:

> Still others, like seed sown among thorns, hear the word; but the worries of this life, the deceitfulness of wealth and the desires for other things come in and choke the word, making it unfruitful.

> Mark 4:18-19 NIV

Weeds left to grow in a field will eventually threaten the production of a crop. In the same way, the thorns of life can choke out our relationship with God. Satan does his best to make the thorns of life look harmless, so we will go on about our life and let them grow. In his deception he says, "Who doesn't worry about life? Everyone has to make a living. Besides, if you are wealthy, you could do a lot of good with your money." Those clever lines are just a sales pitch for the favor of the world. The favor of God is what we need to live fruitful lives.

How motivated we are by God's grace (favor) to say no to the favor of the world depends on our understanding of grace and how much we value it. In Romans 6 and 7, Paul taught important lessons about grace and overcoming sin. We will look in detail at what he said. He began by posing an important question:

---

103. BDAG, p.1054.

> What shall we say, then? Shall we go on sinning so that grace [*charis*] may increase? By no means! We died to sin; how can we live in it any longer?
>
> Romans 6:1-2 NIV

As a result of God's favor, our sins are forgiven, but continuing to sin will not lead to more favor. It makes no sense to live a sinful life as a Christian. That is the wrong way to think about grace. Paul continued:

> Or don't you know that all of us who were baptized into Christ Jesus were baptized into his death? We were therefore buried with him through baptism into death in order that, just as Christ was raised from the dead through the glory of the Father, we too may live a new life.
>
> Romans 6:3-4 NIV

Through baptism, we are buried with Christ into death—death to sin. Then we are raised to a new life. Paul explained the significance of that fact:

> For we know that our old self was crucified with him so that the body of sin might be done away with, that we should <u>no longer be slaves to sin</u>-- because anyone who has died has been <u>freed from sin</u>. [Emphasis added.]
>
> Romans 6:6-7 NIV

We are given a new life. We are like slaves who have been given a chance to be set free—free from the control of our sinful nature. We can say no to ungodliness where before we could not. This is great news. So how should we respond?

> Therefore do not let sin reign in your mortal body so that you obey its evil desires. Do not offer the parts of your body to sin, as instruments of wickedness, but rather <u>offer yourselves to God, as those who have been brought from death to life</u>; and offer the parts of your body to him as instruments of righteousness. For <u>sin shall not be your master</u>, because <u>you are not under law, but under grace</u> [*charis*]. [Emphasis added.]
>
> Romans 6:12-14 NIV

Slaves did not get to choose whom they would serve, and were forced to do what they were told. Paul reminded his readers that sin had that kind of power over them when they lived under the law. But because they had died to their sins, they were no longer under the law, but under grace. And they were free to offer themselves to God.

> What then? Shall we sin because we are not under law but under grace? By no means! Don't you know that when you offer yourselves to someone to obey him as slaves, you are slaves to the one whom you obey--whether you are slaves to sin, which leads to death, or to obedience, which leads to righteousness? [Emphasis added.]
>
> Romans 6:15-16 NIV

As we saw in the chapter on grace and the law, Paul was not advocating that they ignore God's commands; he was urging them to obey them for the right reason. Paul explains that letting God's favor become an excuse to sin, after being given the power to overcome it, would be like a former slave going back to the master he served as a slave to ask if he could be his slave again. If he had been able to win his freedom, why would he ever choose to go back?

> Just as you used to offer the parts of your body in slavery to impurity and to ever-increasing wickedness, so now offer them in slavery to righteousness leading to holiness. When you were slaves to sin, you were free from the control of righteousness. What benefit did you reap at that time from the things you are now ashamed of? Those things result in death! But now that you have been set free from sin and have become slaves to God, the benefit you reap leads to holiness, and the result is eternal life. For the wages of sin is death, but the gift [*charisma*] of God is eternal life in Christ Jesus our Lord.
>
> Romans 6:19b-23 NIV

Just like Paul's readers, we have a choice between a life of ever-increasing wickedness and shame leading to death, or freedom from sin, which leads to holiness and eternal life. Death would be a fair and reasonable payment for our sins; eternal life is a total and complete gift (*charisma*) of God.

> **Definition of *charisma*:** 1. that which is freely and graciously given, *favor bestowed, gift.*[104]

By the favor of God, we get to offer ourselves to Him and be free from the control of sin. When you clear away the confusion caused by the corruption of the world, the better choice becomes obvious.

Then Paul continued; not only did the death of Jesus free them from the control of sin, it released them from all obligations under Jewish law. It was like when a husband or wife dies: their spouse is then free to remarry.[105] By dying to their sin, they were released from the old way of the written code (the law) so they could serve in the new way of the Spirit.[106]

Paul's argument was thorough and persuasive. The law showed them how desperately they needed God.[107] To help them understand how powerless they were under the law, Paul used himself as an example:

> We know that the law is spiritual; but I am unspiritual, sold as a slave to sin. I do not understand what I do. For what I want to do I do not do, but what I hate I do. And if I do what I do not want to do, I agree that the law is good. As it is, it is no longer I myself who do it, but it is sin living in me. I know that nothing good lives in me, that is, in my sinful nature. For I have the desire to do what is good, but I cannot carry it out.
>
> Romans 7:14-18

Paul had been one of the most zealous Jews, but the law gave him no power over his sinful nature. Paul equated his struggle to overcome his sinful nature with slavery. A slave is powerless to win his freedom. No matter how well he does what is asked of him today, tomorrow he

---

104. <u>BDAG</u>, p.1081.
105. Romans 7:2-3
106. Romans 7:6
107. Romans 7:7-13

will still be a slave. Then Paul compared living a powerless life under the law to being in prison:

> …I see another law at work in the members of my body, waging war against the law of my mind and making me a prisoner of the law of sin at work within my members. What a wretched man I am! Who will rescue me from this body of death? Thanks be to God--through Jesus Christ our Lord!
>
> Romans 7:23-25a NIV

A prisoner is subject to what the law says and has no power to win his freedom. In the same way, without Jesus, Paul had no power over his sinful nature and no way to break free. But Jesus did for Paul what neither he nor the Jewish law could do. The death sentence is lifted for anyone in Christ Jesus.

Some people have a different view of Romans 7:14-25 from what I have just described. They believe Paul was describing his battle with sin as a Christian. But that would not make any sense, given all that Paul wrote in Romans 6 about being freed from the control of sin. A Christian who feels he has no control over his sinful nature is living a powerless life. We have been freed from the slavery of sin through our death, burial and resurrection in Jesus. With that in mind, let's reread the passage we read at the beginning of this chapter. This time we will use the NASB translation:

> For the grace of God has appeared, bringing salvation to all men, instructing [*paideuo*] us to deny ungodliness and worldly desires and to live sensibly [*sophronos*], righteously and godly in the present age.
>
> Titus 2:11-12 NASB

Our focus here is on the instruction we get because of God's grace, not the role grace plays in our salvation. The Greek word translated "teaches" (NIV) or "instructing" (NASB) is *paideuo*. In the NASB, it is translated with the following English words (number of times in parenthesis): correcting (1), discipline (2), disciplined (2), disciplines (1), educated (2), instructing (1), punish (2), punished (1), taught (1).

Definition of *paideuo*: 1. to provide instruction for informed and responsible living, *educate*; 2. to assist in the development of a person's ability to make appropriate choices, *practice discipline*.[108]

The writer of Hebrews uses *paideuo* and two words that are based on *paideuo* a total of eight times in the following passage:

> "My son, do not regard lightly the <u>discipline</u> [*paideia*] of the Lord, nor faint when you are reproved by Him; for those whom the Lord loves He <u>disciplines</u> [*paideuo*], and He scourges every son whom He receives." It is for <u>discipline</u> [*paideia*] that you endure; God deals with you as with sons; for what son is there whom *his* father does not <u>discipline</u> [*paideuo*]? But if you are without <u>discipline</u> [*paideia*], of which all have become partakers, then you are illegitimate children and not sons. Furthermore, we had earthly fathers to <u>discipline</u> [*paideutes*] us, and we respected them; shall we not much rather be subject to the Father of spirits, and live? For they <u>disciplined</u> [*paideuo*] us for a short time as seemed best to them, but He *disciplines us* for *our* good, so that we may share His holiness. All <u>discipline</u> [*paideia*] for the moment seems not to be joyful, but sorrowful; yet to those who have been trained by it, afterwards it yields the peaceful fruit of righteousness. [Emphasis added.]
>
> Hebrews 12:5-11 NASB

Definition of *paideia*: 1. the act of providing guidance for responsible living, *upbringing, training, instruction*; 2. the state of being brought up properly, *training*.[109]

A *paideutes* is an instructor or teacher and *paideia* is what a teacher does. But *paideuo* involves much more than the teaching of rules; it also includes correction, guidance, and discipline. Like when a father disciplines his son, God is training us in how to say no to ungodliness. This training is beneficial, though at times it may be unpleasant. But

---

108.   <u>BDAG</u>, p.749.

109.   <u>BDAG</u>, pp.748-749.

it is necessary for us in developing our convictions. It is also a mark of being a child of God. By his grace, God is training us to live "sensibly, righteously and godly," or as the NIV reads, "self-controlled, upright and godly lives."

The Greek word translated as "sensibly" in Titus 2:12 is *sophronos*. This word takes some extra consideration to appreciate.

Definition of *sophronos*: pertaining to being prudent, *soberly, moderately, showing self-control.*[110]

Sophronos is a form of the word *sophron*. Titus 2:12 is the only place in the New Testament where *sophronos* is used, but *sophron* appears in four verses as "prudent" or "sensible" (NASB).

Definition of *sophron*: pertaining to being in control of oneself, *prudent, thoughtful, self-controlled.*[111]

To go a step further, *sophron* comes from the Greek words *sozo* (saving, preserving or rescuing something) and *phren* (thinking or understanding). Living sensibly begins with our thoughts, and requires that we think about things in a way that will preserve what is good. We need to think about how to be safe and avoid things that can harm us. We could describe this as safe thinking. That is a helpful way of looking at it because Satan will do all he can to make dangerous thinking look harmless. He offers fine-sounding arguments for why it is okay to say yes to worldly passions and desires, and he has clever ways of getting us to rationalize our sins.

Satan's arguments can sound very convincing. For example, "You have said no a lot lately, it's time you get to say yes." Or how about "You will feel better if you say yes," or "Nothing bad will happen"? He plays into our self-pity with excuses such as "The reason you cannot say no is because of your past," or "Given all you've been through, you cannot be expected to say no." The classic deception is "'No' is what you want it to be." Then if all else fails, Satan will appear to concede

---

110.   BDAG, p.987.

111.   BDAG, p.987.

defeat: "Okay, you can say no anytime you want, but it does not have to be right now."

Helping us know how we ought to think is part of the favor of God. Without His guidance, it would be easy to go down a path that leads in the opposite direction from God. Here are some of the many scriptures that help us know how we ought to think:

> Set your minds on things above, not on earthly things.
>
> Colossians 3:2 NIV

> Therefore, prepare your minds for action; be self-controlled; set your hope fully on the grace to be given you when Jesus Christ is revealed.
>
> 1 Peter 1:13a NIV

> We demolish arguments and every pretension that sets itself up against the knowledge of God, and we take captive every thought to make it obedient to Christ.
>
> 2 Corinthians 10:5 NIV

God prepares us for the battles that will inevitably come and equips us to fight effectively when they do. One way we fight is by saying no to letting things enter our minds that will destroy us. What we watch on television or look at in magazines or on the internet can corrupt our thinking. How we entertain ourselves at the movies or elsewhere will have a lasting impact. We simply cannot fill our minds with godless entertainment and expect to be able to say no to ungodliness. We need King David's convictions: "I will set before my eyes no vile thing."[112] To protect ourselves from the world, we must minimize its influence whenever we can, including the influence of the people around us.

> Do not be misled: "Bad company corrupts good character."
>
> 1 Corinthians 15:33 NIV

We cannot always control what we see or who we spend time with, and Satan can tempt us when we least expect it, but God will help us

---

112.   Psalms 101:3 NIV

in these times too. He shows his favor by giving us a way to escape our temptations without sinning:

> No temptation has seized you except what is common to man. And God is faithful; he will not let you be tempted beyond what you can bear. But when you are tempted, he will also provide a way out so that you can stand up under it.

1 Corinthians 10:13 NIV

First, God is faithful and will not let you be tempted beyond what you can bear. The temptation may be strong, but you will be able to resist it. Second, God will provide a way out. The NASB reads "way of escape." God will give you an escape route, but you will have to look for it to find it. Third, the way out that God provides may not look good if you are looking for a way to avoid suffering. In fact, if you insist on a pain-free solution, you will probably not even see it as a way out. (By the way, doing without the pleasures of sin is *not* suffering.)

What Paul wrote is not just for the most mature Christians, and is not something we have to grow into. It is for all of us. In fact, you may find that you are already taking the way out in one way or another every day. We often face temptations that we quickly say no to and move on. There are times, however, when we must look harder for the way out. But no matter what the temptation, God promises to give us a way out. This is one of the ways he shows us his favor. We must faithfully look for it, then take it.

To help us say no to ungodliness, God not only gives us a way out of our temptations, he also gives us his Holy Spirit. We receive this gift at baptism.[113] The Holy Spirit helps us in many ways. In our battle with sin, it helps us change our thinking and set our minds on pleasing God:

> Those who live according to the sinful nature have their minds set on what that nature desires; but those who live in accordance with the Spirit have their minds set on what the

---

113. Acts 2:38

> Spirit desires. The mind of sinful man is death, but the mind
> controlled by the Spirit is life and peace; the sinful mind is
> hostile to God. It does not submit to God's law, nor can it do
> so. Those controlled by the sinful nature cannot please God.
>
> Romans 8:5-8 NIV

The Spirit helps us wrest control of our lives away from our sinful
nature. It changes how we think and what we value most, and helps
us submit to God's will for our lives. The Holy Spirit will also be the
power that raises us from the dead:

> You, however, are controlled not by the sinful nature but
> by the Spirit, if the Spirit of God lives in you. And if any-
> one does not have the Spirit of Christ, he does not belong to
> Christ. But if Christ is in you, your body is dead because of
> sin, yet your spirit is alive because of righteousness. And if
> the Spirit of him who raised Jesus from the dead is living in
> you, he who raised Christ from the dead will also give life to
> your mortal bodies through his Spirit, who lives in you.
>
> Romans 8:9-11 NIV

The Spirit helps us stop being a slave to sin:

> Therefore, brothers, we have an obligation--but it is not to the
> sinful nature, to live according to it. <u>For if you live accord-
> ing to the sinful nature, you will die</u>; but if <u>by the Spirit you
> put to death the misdeeds of the body, you will live</u>, because
> those who are led by the Spirit of God are sons of God. For
> you did not receive a spirit that makes you a slave again to
> fear, but you received the Spirit of sonship. And by him we
> cry, "Abba, Father." [Emphasis added.]
>
> Romans 8:12-15 NIV

Several times in Romans 6, 7 and 8, Paul makes the point that
if you let your sinful nature continue to rule over your life, you will
die. But if you overcome your sins by the Spirit, you will live. God's
Holy Spirit is an important part of our defense against sin. That is why
Paul told the Galatians to keep in step with the Spirit. The fruit of

the Spirit in our lives is love, joy, peace, patience, kindness, goodness, faithfulness, gentleness and self-control.[114]

The Holy Spirit is yet another example of God's graciousness toward us. Not only does the Spirit fill our lives with things we need, the Spirit helps us have self-control and say no to ungodliness. Despite our best efforts, however, we will still lose some battles with Satan. That should not surprise us because scriptures warn us that Satan is filled with fury, and is at war with anyone who wants to obey God.[115] Peter described Satan as a roaring lion looking for someone to devour.[116] But God is gracious and his word helps us at these moments too:

> Therefore confess your sins to each other and pray for each other so that you may be healed. The prayer of a righteous man is powerful and effective.
>
> James 5:16 NIV

> If we claim to have fellowship with him yet walk in the darkness, we lie and do not live by the truth. But if we walk in the light, as he is in the light, we have fellowship with one another, and the blood of Jesus, his Son, purifies us from all sin.

> If we claim to be without sin, we deceive ourselves and the truth is not in us. If we confess our sins, he is faithful and just and will forgive us our sins and purify us from all unrighteousness.
>
> 1 John 1:6-9 NIV

These verses give us practical direction on how to fight our battle with sin. No one can claim to be without sin. But we are no longer a slave to our sin. We can combat Satan's influence and our sinful nature by being humble and open about our sins. Then the blood of Jesus will purify us and God will forgive us. We get to leave our sins behind.

---

114. Galatians 5:22-23

115. Revelations 12:12-17

116. 1 Peter 5:8

God's favor is our greatest motivation for saying no to worldliness. He sent Jesus to pay the ransom price for our sins; He gave us his Holy Spirit to guide us; and He continues to purify us as we walk in the light. Let's look for the way out when we are tempted to sin, and be humble and open when we fail. What awaits us in heaven is well worth whatever it takes to say "no" to ungodliness and worldly desires.

WORKSHEET 8 – Grace Teaches Us to Say "No"

1. In general, what helps Christians to not go on sinning?

_____

_____

_____

_____

_____

_____

_____

_____

_____

_____

2. More specifically, how does God's favor teach us to say no to ungodliness and the favor of the world?

_____

_____

_____

_____

_____

_____

_____

_____

_____

_____

_____

_____

3. What are some of the ways God provides us a way out when we are tempted?

_____

_____

_____

_____

_____

_____

_____

_____

_____

4. According to Romans 8, in what ways do we benefit from having the Holy Spirit?

_____

_____

_____

_____

_____

_____

_____

_____

_____

_____

Chapter Notes:

Chapter 9

God's Grace is Enough

> To keep me from becoming conceited because of these sur-
> passingly great revelations, there was given me a thorn in
> my flesh, a messenger of Satan, to torment me. Three times
> I pleaded with the Lord to take it away from me. But he said
> to me, "My grace is sufficient for you, for my power is made
> perfect in weakness…"
>
> 2 Corinthians 12:7-9a NIV

These few words give us valuable insight into how to think about those things we cannot change without God's help. Paul did not mention what his thorn in the flesh was. This was perhaps because his readers already knew. Or perhaps he did not want them to get sidetracked by comparing their own situations to what he was dealing with, and miss learning a valuable lesson. People have offered different theories about what tormented Paul, but not knowing keeps us from comparing our thorns to Paul's. If we knew what Paul's thorn was, we might conclude that our thorn was different, and that the lesson Paul learned does not apply. But it does apply, and God's grace (favor) is sufficient, no matter how unique or how difficult our situation may be.

Paul described his thorn as a messenger of Satan. He didn't say Satan caused it, only that Satan used it as a way to torment him. The Greek word translated as "torment" is *kolaphizo*.

Definition of *kolaphizo*: 1. to strike sharply, especially with the hand, *strike with the fist, beat, cuff*; 2. to cause physical impairment, *torment*.[117]

Have you ever felt tormented by a weakness? When Satan uses something to attack us, we can feel like we are being punched with a fist. He punches us to get us to sin, and miss out on the power of God. With one blow he says, "You failed." With another he says, "You might as well give up now because you will never be able to do it." With yet another blow, he tempts us to look for relief from trials in all the wrong places. In general, Satan wants us to seek comfort in the favor of the world instead of the favor of God.

Paul wrote that the thorn in his flesh was a messenger of Satan. I picture the bicycle-riding messengers in big cities who weave through traffic and dodge pedestrians to deliver packages door-to-door. Satan has a similar mode of operation. He finds a way through the busyness and challenges of life to deliver personalized attacks to your doorstep. Have you received any of his packages lately?

To describe someone in your life that you find annoying, you may have said, "He is a thorn in my side." That metaphor communicates that he is painful for you to deal with. If you have ever been stuck by a thorn, you know that such pain is impossible to ignore. So we can understand how Paul felt, and why he repeatedly pleaded with God to make it go away. When we are struggling with our thorns, we naturally wonder why this is happening to us. Paul reasoned that his thorn was to help him be humble. Our reasoning could be something like this: "I should not have to put up with this thorn because it keeps me from doing things that I really want to do for God. Without it, I could accomplish so much more, so God should take it away. If God would just do this, life would be good."

Do we really know what is best for us? How well do we understand what we need? Are we not better off with God in control so *his* power can be made perfect in *our* weakness? Our biggest need is not getting rid of our thorns; it is having God's favor in our lives.

---

117. <u>BDAG</u>, p.555.

God's answer to Paul's request was not what he wanted to hear, but God was not punishing Paul or just being mean. Instead, God wanted Paul to know that he already had what he needed. God's power is made perfect in weakness. We need to remind ourselves of this whenever we are wondering why God does not do something for us that we think would be good. We must also remember that we do not have to eliminate our pain or hardship to be valuable to God.

The Greek word translated as "sufficient" in the phrase, "my grace is sufficient" is *arkeo*.

Definition of *arkeo*: 1. *be enough, sufficient, adequate*; 2. *be satisfied/content with something.*[118]

"Sufficient" does not mean that God's grace is barely enough. It means we will not be found lacking if we have God's grace. The application for Paul was that he had what he needed to serve God and ward off Satan's attacks. When our weaknesses threaten to stop our progress, God's favor is all we need to move forward. It is sufficient. In Philippians 4:12, Paul wrote that he had learned the secret of being content. I believe his secret was having the favor of God. We can be content if we trust God to know what is best for us. And when we might otherwise feel weak, we can be strong if we let God's grace make up the difference.

We certainly cannot blame Paul for asking repeatedly that his thorn be taken away. Jesus even encouraged it when he taught about the widow who persisted in prayer.[119] But, like Paul, when we do not get the answer we are looking for, we must let God's grace be sufficient.

It is not easy to consistently feel up to the challenges in our lives. We can feel strong and victorious one day, then feel weak and overwhelmed the next. We can be faithless in the evening, and wake up the next morning feeling faithful. When we tire of the spiritual battle, we can think of ways that God could (and should) give us more (or less) of something that would make our battle easier to win. And when we are

---

118.   BDAG, pp.131-132.

119.   Luke 18:1-5

embarrassed by a weakness or discouraged because nothing seems to be going as planned, it can be a challenge to be happy. Why didn't God bless my perfect solution? We have to learn the same lesson that Paul had to learn—God's grace is enough. Having His favor in our lives will ensure that we have what we need.

As it turned out, Paul's weaknesses didn't limit him that much. With God's favor, Paul inspired many people to become Christians and wrote almost half of the New Testament. And in the end, Paul saw the value of his weaknesses:

> Therefore I will boast all the more gladly about my weaknesses, so that Christ's power may rest on me. That is why, for Christ's sake, I delight in weaknesses, in insults, in hardships, in persecutions, in difficulties. For when I am weak, then I am strong.
>
> 2 Corinthians 12:9b-10 NIV

We should not feel defeated by our thorns in the flesh. We can face challenges and still have God's favor. And we are no less valuable to God when we are weak, if our weaknesses lead us to rely more on God. His power is made perfect in weakness. God's grace is more than enough!

WORKSHEET 9 – God's Grace is Enough

1. Are you dealing with a thorn of your own? How has Satan tried to use it against you, and how does God's favor help you deal with it?

_____

_____

_____

_____

_____

_____

2. What lessons did Paul learn from dealing with his thorn in the flesh?

_____

_____

_____

_____

_____

_____

3. How does having the favor of God help you be content in all circumstances?

_____

_____

_____

_____

_____

_____

Chapter Notes:

Chapter 10

The Favor to Suffer

> For it has been granted [*charizomai*] to you on behalf of Christ not only to believe on him, but also to suffer for him.
>
> Philippians 1:29 NIV

God's favor brings many useful things into our lives, but we would not expect suffering to be one of them. Suffering on behalf of Christ, however, is a key part of the favor of God. Not only is it a privilege to know Jesus and experience the blessings he brings into our lives, it is a privilege to suffer for him.

As mentioned in Chapter 1, the Greek word *charizomai,* translated as "granted" in Philippians 1:29, means "to give freely as a favor, give graciously."[120] To show his favor, God gave us the privilege of suffering on behalf of Christ. This takes some thought to appreciate. Typically, having privileges means that we enjoy perks or preferential treatment, and a favor is something good. But God's wisdom is much different than man's wisdom, and in God's kingdom we are blessed when we suffer for Jesus.

This is not to say that all suffering is part of the favor of God. The suffering that is part of the favor of God is the suffering we endure for Jesus. There are several ways this may occur. Following Jesus and striving to be like him can bring a variety of challenges into your life. If you

---

120. BDAG, p.1078.

live a godly life, you will be persecuted.[121] Sharing your faith, taking an unpopular stand for Jesus, or drawing a line on what you will or won't do, can set you apart from the crowd. It may even test the bond of a friendship, impact your career, or influence where you choose to live. If God chooses to use you to accomplish his greater plan, it probably will involve suffering. Joseph's hardships, for example, were part of God's plan to save his family.[122] Esther's suffering saved the Jewish nation. Many of the faithful people honored in Hebrews 11 suffered after being drafted into God's service. You may even deliberately put yourself through suffering because you are determined to change something in your life or say no to sin.

Suffering for Jesus may not look like a privilege, but the Bible gives us several reasons why it is. Still, it would be nice if we could learn what we need to know about suffering by just reading about it in our Bibles, or by listening to people describe how they endured it, instead of having to learn it from personal experience. But it just does not work that way. There are benefits to suffering that we do not receive unless we go through it.

Suffering develops perseverance:

> Consider it pure joy, my brothers, whenever you face trials of many kinds, because you know that the testing of your faith develops perseverance. Perseverance must finish its work so that you may be mature and complete, not lacking anything.
>
> James 1:2-4 NIV

The trials James refers to have a beneficial purpose.[123] They are not the kind of trials we bring on ourselves by disobeying God; these are the ones that will help us grow spiritually and get to heaven. They develop in us the perseverance we need to stay faithful until we are able to be with God. Many Christians, however, compromise on their convictions when they encounter suffering for Jesus. Others stop growing spiritu-

---

121. 2 Timothy 3:12

122. Genesis 45:5

123. According to Vine, the Greek word *peirasmos,* translated as "trials," denotes a trial with a beneficial purpose, one that is divinely permitted or sent.

ally because they see themselves as a victim of circumstances instead of someone who needs to persevere. Some have even given up their faith entirely because they were unwilling to suffer, even for Jesus.

Can you see a purpose for the suffering you have experienced? Sometimes it is not obvious. Job, for example, who faced health issues, the loss of loved ones, and financial loss, was not told why he had to endure suffering. In the end, though, he realized how God used it to build his faith.[124] He was also an example for his friends. Job is known for his perseverance and how he remained faithful to God. Eternity was more important to Job than his day-to-day comfort.

To consider trials "pure joy," we must understand that the divine purpose of our trials is to help us get to heaven. Trials test our faith, and we know we need that, but our nature is to want to be in control of our lives and eliminate all suffering. We tend to focus more on finding relief than on finding faith. But God can work through our trials if we persevere. Then we will develop more faith. God gives us relief in many ways every day, but we need faith more than we need relief.

Suffering produces character:

Good character is another quality produced by persevering through suffering. It often takes some form of pressure to develop one's character. Paul knew this from extensive personal experience. He described how suffering led to other things he could rejoice about:

> …And we rejoice in the hope of the glory of God. Not only so, but we also rejoice in our sufferings, because we know that suffering produces perseverance; perseverance, character [*dokime*]; and character [*dokime*], hope. And hope does not disappoint us, because God has poured out his love into our hearts by the Holy Spirit, whom he has given us.
>
> Romans 5:2b-5 NIV

The Greek word translated "character" is *dokime*. In the NASB, it is translated as "proven character."

---

124. Job 42:5

Definition of *dokime*: 1. the process or means of determining the genuineness of something, *testing, means of testing*; 2. genuineness as a result of a test, *genuine, without alloy.*[125]

We develop *dokime* when we respond to challenging situations in ways that please God. For example, when my sons faced tough situations in grade school, we would ask them what they thought God would want them to learn from it. What could they learn from getting the toughest teacher or being teased or bullied by a classmate on the playground? When they thought about it awhile, they could usually find something they could learn to help them face their challenges in a way that would please God. In the same way, our challenges will help us develop our character.

Suffering produces hope:

Suffering forces us to re-examine what is important to us. Is it worth it to me to endure all this suffering? If the answer is yes, then we will persevere through the suffering and have an opportunity to develop more perseverance, character and hope. Hope is another quality we gain through suffering. It is counter-intuitive that hope is produced by the same things that require perseverance, but understanding that point can open our eyes to how it happens.

> I pray also that the eyes of your heart may be enlightened in order that <u>you may know the hope to which he has called you</u>, the riches of his glorious inheritance in the saints, and his incomparably great power for us who believe. That power is like the working of his mighty strength. [Emphasis added.]
>
> Ephesians 1:18-19 NIV

Paul used words like *riches, glorious, incomparable* and *mighty* to paint a picture of what life looked like to him. This is not how most people would feel if they faced trials that were similar to Paul's. Our spiritual eyes have to be open for us to see things in the way Paul did. Otherwise, suffering would more likely produce frustration, bitterness or even despair.

---

125. <u>BDAG</u>, p.256.

Hope helps us endure, makes us bold, and helps us be patient.[126] Hope gives us a new perspective on life that we could not get any other way.

> Therefore we do not lose heart. Though outwardly we are wasting away, yet inwardly we are being renewed day by day. For our light and momentary troubles are achieving for us an eternal glory that far outweighs them all. So we fix our eyes not on what is seen, but on what is unseen. For what is seen is temporary, but what is unseen is eternal.
>
> 2 Corinthians 4:16-18 NIV

My body reminds me often of the fact that we are wasting away, but God helps me remember that today's suffering is temporary and tomorrow's glory is eternal.

Suffering teaches us to rely on God:

When the Lord sent Ananias to Paul in Damascus, the Lord told Ananias, "I will show him how much he must suffer for my name."[127] Paul found that to be true. He was flogged, beaten, stoned, shipwrecked, put in prison, and often went without sleep, food, heat and clothing.[128] But Paul saw how his suffering served a purpose and was part of the favor of God:

> We do not want you to be uninformed, brothers, about the hardships we suffered in the province of Asia. We were under great pressure, far beyond our ability to endure, so that we despaired even of life. Indeed, in our hearts we felt the sentence of death. But this happened that we might not rely on ourselves but on God, who raises the dead. He has delivered us from such a deadly peril, and he will deliver us. On him we have set our hope that he will continue to deliver us, as you help us by your prayers. Then many will give thanks on

---

126.   2 Corinthians 3:12; Romans 8:25

127.   Acts 9:16

128.   2 Corinthians 11:23-28

our behalf for the gracious favor [*charisma*][129] granted us in
answer to the prayers of many.

2 Corinthians 1:8-11 NIV

Paul described a desperate situation that was comparable to being
sentenced to death. How could it serve a useful purpose? Paul concluded that God was helping him not rely on himself. Gaining relief from
his severe suffering would have seemed valuable to Paul, but learning
to rely more on God was priceless.

Despite suffering for his service to God, Paul felt God's favor in
the most severe trial. He came to a rather bold conclusion about the
purpose of all his suffering:

> Now I rejoice in what was suffered for you, and I fill up in my
> flesh what is still lacking in regard to Christ's afflictions, for
> the sake of his body, which is the church.

Colossians 1:24 NIV

Paul claimed that his suffering filled up something that was lacking in the suffering of Jesus. His reasoning could have been something
like this: When Jesus was crucified, the work He began was not fin-
ished. So by taking up where Jesus left off, and carrying on the work
of strengthening and helping the church to grow, Paul was sharing in
the work Christ began. And if he happened to suffer while sharing in
that work, he was completing the suffering of Christ.[130] Having that
perspective would make a big difference in Paul's willingness to suffer.
Paul did not shrink back when he suffered for taking a stand for Jesus:

> And of this gospel I was appointed a herald and an apostle
> and a teacher. That is why I am suffering as I am. Yet I am
> not ashamed, because I know whom I have believed, and am
> convinced that he is able to guard what I have entrusted to
> him for that day.

2 Timothy 1:11-12 NIV

---

129. *Charisma* is a gift freely and graciously given. It is taken from *charizomai*, showing favor or giving freely. *Charizomai* is from *charis*, the word translated as "favor" or "grace." (BDAG, p.1081).

130. Barclay

Even when he was jailed like a criminal, Paul was convinced that God would take care of him. "I know whom I have believed." This statement is significant. Paul formerly persecuted anyone who claimed to follow Jesus, but now he is connected in the most personal way. This says a lot about the love Jesus had for Paul and Paul's humility.

Paul understood and felt God's favor in his life. He considered it a privilege to take an unpopular stand for Jesus and carry on His work. Paul expressed his desire to know Christ and the power of his resurrection and the fellowship of sharing in his sufferings.[131] He found out that knowing Christ includes knowing how he would be able to endure suffering. It would be difficult, if not impossible, to keep a man with this mind-set from preaching the gospel!

We can learn more about the benefits of suffering for Jesus and see how it can transform someone's life by looking at Peter's life. When he left his fishing nets to follow Jesus, he had a long way to go to become a fearless man of God. But from Peter's own words, we see how he grew in his willingness to suffer for Jesus. In his early years, he did all he could to avoid suffering. Shortly before Jesus was crucified, Jesus told Peter and the other disciples that He would have to suffer and die in Jerusalem. This was Peter's response:

> Peter took him aside and began to rebuke him. "Never, Lord!" he said. "This shall never happen to you!"
>
> Jesus turned and said to Peter, "Get behind me, Satan! You are a stumbling block to me; you do not have in mind the things of God, but the things of men."
>
> Matthew 16:22-23 NIV

To Peter, it did not make sense that Jesus should suffer. Jesus had done nothing wrong. But to Peter's surprise, Jesus turned to him and said, "Get behind me, Satan!" Jesus recognized that Satan was using Peter's words to dissuade him from going to the cross. Then Jesus told

---

131. Philippians 3:10

his disciples that they too would have to deny themselves and take up their cross and follow Him.[132]

On the night Jesus was arrested, Jesus told Peter that he would disown Him three times. Peter again argued with Jesus and even claimed that he was willing to die for Him. (Peter was about to learn a profound lesson.) Then when Jesus was arrested, Peter followed at a distance, hoping to not be noticed. But when confronted, he vehemently denied that he even knew Jesus. Then the rooster crowed, and the Lord looked right at Peter. Peter went out and wept bitterly.[133]

Jesus was crucified and three days later rose from the dead, but Peter was still struggling. Peter and the other disciples had gone fishing, so Jesus went out to meet them and had this exchange with Peter:

> When they had finished eating, Jesus said to Simon Peter, "Simon son of John, do you truly love me more than these?" "Yes, Lord," he said, "you know that I love you." Jesus said, "Feed my lambs." Again Jesus said, "Simon son of John, do you truly love me?" He answered, "Yes, Lord, you know that I love you." Jesus said, "Take care of my sheep." The third time he said to him, "Simon son of John, do you love me?" Peter was hurt because Jesus asked him the third time, "Do you love me?" He said, "Lord, you know all things; you know that I love you." Jesus said, "Feed my sheep. I tell you the truth, when you were younger you dressed yourself and went where you wanted; but when you are old you will stretch out your hands, and someone else will dress you and lead you where you do not want to go." Jesus said this to indicate the kind of death by which Peter would glorify God. Then he said to him, "Follow me!"
>
> John 21:15-19 NIV

It appears that Peter is still sorting out what the recent events would mean for his life. Should he go back to fishing or leave his nets a second time to follow Jesus? Jesus asked Peter some questions to bring him to a decision: What do you love? Is it fishing or me? If it is me, then take

132. Matthew 16:24

133. Luke 22:61-62

care of my church. After two more exchanges, Jesus told Peter: Loving me will lead you to die for me.

Evidently the things Jesus said stirred Peter's heart and reminded him that his relationship with Jesus would be worth it. He decided that he would follow Jesus, even if it meant he would suffer greatly. Soon after, Peter and the other disciples began to preach boldly. They eventually were arrested, threatened and flogged. But instead of running away, they boldly proclaimed their allegiance to Jesus. They even rejoiced that they were counted worthy to suffer for His name.[134] Unlike before, Peter was willing to suffer for Jesus. Later, he wrote the following:

> Who is going to harm you if you are eager to do good? But even if you should suffer for what is right, you are blessed. "Do not fear what they fear; do not be frightened."
>
> 1 Peter 3:13-14 NIV

Fear was what caused Peter to deny Jesus three times, but here he writes that if you suffer for doing what is right, you are blessed. Peter's transformation into a courageous man and his willingness to follow Jesus at any cost gives us hope!

Suffering proves your faith:

It took awhile for Peter, but he eventually understood and valued the blessings that trials brought into his life:

> In this you greatly rejoice, though now for a little while you may have had to suffer grief in all kinds of trials. These have come so that your faith--of greater worth than gold, which perishes even though refined by fire--may be proved genuine and may result in praise, glory and honor when Jesus Christ is revealed. Though you have not seen him, you love him; and even though you do not see him now, you believe in him and are filled with an inexpressible and glorious joy, for you are receiving the goal of your faith, the salvation of your souls. [Emphasis added.]
>
> 1 Peter 1:6-9 NIV

---

134. Acts 5:41

It is a paradox that we can be facing trials and still be filled with an inexpressible joy. The only way this can happen is for our faith to be worth more to us than gold. If that is the case, we will welcome anything that increases our faith. (Otherwise we would prefer things that increase our gold.) Suffering proves our faith. What could be more valuable? This helps explain why Peter and the other apostles left the Sanhedrin rejoicing after being flogged for refusing to stop teaching about Jesus.[135]

Suffering for Jesus is commendable by God:

> For it is commendable [*charis*] if a man bears up under the pain of unjust suffering because he is conscious of God. But how is it to your credit if you receive a beating for doing wrong and endure it? But if you suffer for doing good and you endure it, this is commendable [*charis*] before God. To this you were called, because Christ suffered for you, <u>leaving you an example, that you should follow in his steps</u>. [Emphasis added.]
>
> 1 Peter 2:19-21 NIV

When Peter wrote these words, he understood why Jesus told his disciples to deny themselves and take up their cross and follow him. Twice in this passage, we are told that if we suffer to follow Jesus, we will experience the grace of God. The NASB translation reads, "finds favor" for the Greek word *charis* instead of "commendable."

Being called to suffer on behalf of Christ is an act of grace from God. We need to hear that again—suffering is a gift of grace. It is a great privilege to suffer for the one who suffered on our behalf. Jesus endured unjust suffering without complaining or retaliating. Peter found out where Jesus got the strength to endure such suffering:

> "He committed no sin, and no deceit was found in his mouth." When they hurled their insults at him, he did not retaliate; when he suffered, he made no threats. Instead, he <u>entrusted himself to him who judges justly</u>. [Emphasis added.]
>
> 1 Peter 2:21-23 NIV

---

135. Acts 5:41-42 NIV

If we are unwilling to suffer to follow Jesus, the testing of our faith will produce things less positive than perseverance, and leave us without hope. But if we entrust ourselves to God, we can faithfully follow Jesus' example—and that is commendable by God.

We have the right expectations when we understand how suffering on behalf of Jesus is part of the favor of God, and that suffering does not mean something went wrong.

> Dear friends, do not be surprised at the painful trial you are suffering, as though something strange were happening to you. But rejoice that you participate in the sufferings of Christ, so that you may be overjoyed when his glory is revealed.
>
> 1 Peter 4:12-13 NIV

When Jesus was arrested, Peter may have thought that something had gone horribly wrong. But Peter eventually learned that the suffering Jesus went through was part of God's plan. When we encounter suffering, we too can be tempted to think that something must be wrong, believing that we should not be suffering. But trials do not mean that something strange and unusual is happening to us, and we should not be surprised that we suffer. When we encounter unexpected or persistent suffering, however, Satan will try to get us to lose heart and turn back. Satan does not want us to develop perseverance, character and hope. He will try telling us that trials mean that God is against us, or that something has gone wrong because suffering of any kind is bad. He will try to get us to look for relief from our suffering in all the wrong places. His most deceptive weapon may be to get us to think, "I should not have to suffer." He may even use someone you know to deliver that message in the way that he used Peter's words to attack Jesus. Whatever his message, we can say, "Get behind me, Satan."

> Blessed is the man who perseveres under trial, because when he has stood the test, he will receive the crown of life that God has promised to those who love him.
>
> James 1:12 NIV

The crown of life is ahead of you. There will be no more suffering in heaven, and the suffering we go through now to prepare us for that day is part of the favor of God. Trials are part of a refining process that takes a lifetime to complete.

WORKSHEET 10 – The Favor to Suffer

1. Why do you think God calls us to suffer on his behalf?

_____

_____

_____

_____

_____

_____

_____

_____

_____

_____

2. How does knowing that suffering for Jesus is part of the favor of
    God help you endure it?

_____

_____

_____

_____

_____

_____

_____

_____

_____

_____

_____

_____

3. What has suffering produced in your life?

_____

_____

_____

_____

_____

_____

_____

_____

_____

_____

4. How does God's favor help us overcome the fear of suffering for Jesus?

_____

_____

_____

_____

_____

_____

_____

_____

_____

_____

_____

_____

Chapter Notes:

Chapter 11

Be Strong in the Grace

"You therefore, my son, be strong in the grace that is in Christ Jesus."

2 Timothy 2:1 NASB

How we define grace has a significant influence on what we conclude from this scripture. For example, people who think that grace is basically the same as salvation typically conclude that being strong in grace must mean being confident of their salvation. It is true that the scriptures teach us how we can have confidence, but grace is the favor of God, not salvation. God saved us because of his favor; however, his favor encompasses more than our salvation. When Paul encouraged Timothy to be strong in the grace, he had something else in mind.

In a somewhat related matter, a lack of confidence is a major issue for some people. They struggle with not feeling good enough to be accepted by God. For them, being encouraged to "be strong in the grace" may lead to thoughts like "I'm not worried about being strong in it—I just want to know that I have it." Many Christians have doubts and quietly wonder to themselves, "Do I really have God's grace?"

To make matters worse, our pride works against us getting help. We tend to want other people to think we are "strong in the grace," even when we may not be. This leads to us not being open about where we really are, and prevents us from getting stronger. We humans behave in strange ways! Before we can grow stronger in God's grace, however, we have to be willing to admit that this is something we need to do. That takes humility.

God's grace is not a mysterious blessing that we somehow become good enough to receive. In fact, we can have God's grace even when we think we are weak (like Gideon). At the same time, we must not assume that we have the benefit of God's grace, no matter what we do. We must not take God's grace for granted.

> What shall we say then? Are we to continue in sin so that grace may increase? May it never be! How shall we who died to sin still live in it?
>
> Romans 6:1-2 NASB

In so many words, Paul asks, "Do you think God will just show you more favor?" The sacrifice of Jesus was the ultimate act of God's favor—we should not act like we think God should do more. Neither should we let our weakness become an excuse to stop trying to please God. We are called to be strong in the grace, not aim to barely get by. God's grace should make us *more* serious about our relationship with Him, not *less*. Instead of it becoming an excuse to make less effort to be close to God, his favor and the relationship we have as a result should motivate us to do more to please him.

There is an ongoing need and a continual opportunity for Christians to receive grace and mercy from God. These New Testament writers offer encouragement to that effect:

- The writer of Hebrews: "Therefore let us draw near with confidence to the throne of grace, so that we may receive mercy and find grace to help in time of need."[136]

---

136. Hebrews 4:16 NASB

- Peter: "grow in the grace and knowledge of our Lord and Savior Jesus Christ."[137]

- Paul: "Grace, mercy and peace from God the Father and Christ Jesus our Lord."[138]

In thirteen New Testament letters, Paul wished his readers more grace and peace.[139] This is another example where equating grace with salvation can lead to misunderstandings. We are encouraged to grow in grace, but how can we grow in salvation or be strong in salvation? If I am saved today, how can I be *more* saved tomorrow? In reality, it is possible that tomorrow (or the next day) I may feel *less* saved than today, especially if I sin again. This can lead to feeling saved on my best days and lost on all the rest. And when we struggle like this, Satan will do his best to convince us to give up. But grace is God's favor and goodwill, so we understand why Paul wished his readers more grace.

The Greek word translated "strong" in 2 Timothy 2:1 is *endunamoo*.

Definition of *endunamoo*: 1. to cause one to be able to function or do something, *strengthen*; 2. to become able to function or do something, *become strong*.[140]

In other passages in the NASB, *endunamoo* is translated as "grew strong," "increasing in strength," "strengthened" or "strengthens." *Endunamoo* describes what people saw happening to Paul while he was preaching about Jesus in Damascus.

All those hearing him continued to be amazed, and were saying, "Is this not he who in Jerusalem destroyed those who called on this name, and who had come here for the purpose

---

137. 2 Peter 3:18 NASB

138. 1 Timothy 1:2, 2 Timothy 1:2 NASB

139. Romans 1:7, 1 Corinthians 1:3, 2 Corinthians 1:2, Galatians 1:3, Ephesians 1:2, Philippians 1:2, Colossians 1:2, 1 Thessalonians 1:1, 2 Thessalonians 1:2, Titus 1:4 and Philemon 1:3

140. BDAG, p.333.

of bringing them bound before the chief priests?" But Saul kept increasing in <u>strength</u> [*endunamoo*] and confounding the Jews who lived at Damascus by proving that this Jesus is the Christ. [Emphasis added.]

Acts 9:21-22 NASB

The NIV reads, "Saul grew more and more powerful." God empowered Saul (Paul) to prove that Jesus was the Christ. Just days earlier, however, Paul believed that Jesus was only a man. The transformation in Paul was dramatic. In the past, he thought of himself like this:

> If anyone else thinks he has reasons to put confidence in the flesh, I have more: circumcised on the eighth day, of the people of Israel, of the tribe of Benjamin, a Hebrew of Hebrews; in regard to the law, a Pharisee; as for zeal, persecuting the church; as for legalistic righteousness, faultless.

Philippians 3:4b-6 NIV

Unexpectedly, the incident on the road to Damascus led Paul to find out that his confidence was in all the wrong things. All his accomplishments together amounted to worthless legalistic righteousness. Paul's life and ministry were turned upside down. He went from being strong in legalistic righteousness to being strong in God's grace (favor). He no longer took credit for his accomplishments:

> I can do all things through Him who strengthens [*endunamoo*] me.

Philippians 4:13 NASB

> I thank Christ Jesus our Lord, who has strengthened [*endunamoo*] me, because He considered me faithful, putting me into service.

1 Timothy 1:12 NASB

Endunamoo is also the word Paul used to describe what happened to Abraham's faith after learning that he would become the father of many nations.

> Without weakening in his faith, he faced the fact that his body was as good as dead--since he was about a hundred years

old--and that Sarah's womb was also dead. Yet he did not waver through unbelief regarding the promise of God, but was <u>strengthened</u> [*endunamoo*] in his faith and gave glory to God, being fully persuaded that God had power to do what he had promised. [Emphasis added.]

Romans 4:19-21 NIV

Despite evidence that what Abraham hoped for was nearly impossible, Abraham grew strong (*endunamoo*) in his faith. It is often the most difficult situations that lead to the most growth in our faith.

When we consider what it will take to be spiritually strong, most of us think how we should pray more, read our Bibles more, and be more devoted to worship and spiritual relationships. These things are vital to our spiritual growth, but we can do all of them and still not be strong in the grace that is in Christ Jesus. We can do them without considering the impact of the favor of God in our lives.

Abraham grew strong because he relied more and more on the favor of God. Moses was strong in God's grace because, more than anything, he wanted to know God. God knew Moses by name and said He would go with him.[141] The strength Moses demonstrated in his leadership of the Israelites was a result of the favor of God.

Paul knew the value of being strong in the grace that is in Christ Jesus. He put his confidence in knowing Christ.[142] He credited God's grace for changing his life and for his accomplishments:

But by the <u>grace</u> of God I am what I am, and his <u>grace</u> to me was not without effect. No, I worked harder than all of them--yet not I, but the grace of God that was with me. [Emphasis added.]

1 Corinthians 15:10 NIV

Substituting the word "favor" for "grace" in the above passage can bring clarity to the message: "But by the favor of God I am what I am, and his favor to me was not without effect. No, I worked harder

---

141.   Exodus 33:13-14, 17

142.   Philippians 3:7-10

than all of them—yet not I, but the favor of God that was with me." Reading it that way helps us see how the favor of God motivated and enabled Paul to accomplish great things. It was not the hard work that led to God's favor; the hard work was the result. Paul was strong in God's grace.

Becoming strong in God's grace will require spiritual growth. In the following scripture, Peter addressed the need to grow in grace. Notice what you can combat by growing in grace and knowledge:

> Therefore, dear friends, since you already know this, be on your guard so that you may not be carried away by the error of lawless men and fall from your secure position. But <u>grow in the grace and knowledge of our Lord and Savior Jesus Christ</u>. To him be glory both now and forever! Amen. [Emphasis added.]
>
> 2 Peter 3:17-18 NIV

These verses are Peter's last recorded words. The book of 2 Peter contains warnings to Christians about false teachers, scoffers and the second coming of Jesus. Twice he told his readers to make every effort to be godly. He concluded by saying, "Grow in the grace and knowledge of our Lord and Savior Jesus Christ." In the previous chapter about the favor of suffering, we considered Peter's life experiences and how he grew in his convictions about suffering for Jesus. Peter knew the value of spiritual growth, and he called his fellow Christians to grow in grace and knowledge.

We understand what it means to grow in knowledge, but what does it mean to grow in God's grace? We know that Jesus grew in favor (*charis*) with God,[143] but what might that look like for us? I believe it is much like my experience raising two sons. I always wanted them to do well and did everything I could to help them. The more they made good decisions, the more of my favor they experienced. And the more responsible they were, the more freedom they received. In other words, they grew in the grace (favor) of their father. But if they had made bad

---

143. Luke 2:52

decisions and had chosen to live self-centered lives, I would have had fewer opportunities to show them my favor. To be clear, I had no desire to withhold my favor from my sons; receiving my favor depended more on the two of them than on me.

When they turned sixteen, I helped my sons get their driver's licenses. At first they were given opportunities to drive the family car, and eventually I bought a car for them to use. I gave them the necessary amount of supervision and guidelines to follow for safe driving. I knew that my caution was warranted, because of the dangers they faced and the potential for them to harm other people. As they proved themselves, they grew in my favor and enjoyed more benefits.

On one occasion, however, one son completely disregarded my good guidelines and lost his driving privileges for a time. I wanted to bless him, but impressing his friends meant more to him than my favor. So for a short time, he received my favor in the form of discipline. When he repented, he enjoyed more of the blessings of my favor.

The same is true for us. The more we hold to God's word and faithfully obey it, the more he can work in our lives:

> Do not merely listen to the word, and so deceive yourselves. Do what it says. Anyone who listens to the word but does not do what it says is like a man who looks at his face in a mirror and, after looking at himself, goes away and immediately forgets what he looks like. But the man who looks intently into the perfect law that gives freedom, and continues to do this, not forgetting what he has heard, but doing it--he will be blessed in what he does.
>
> James 1:22-25 NIV

In 2 Peter 3:17-18, cited above, Peter warned us that distortions of the scriptures are a threat to our relationship with God. Then he challenged us to combat such influences by growing in the grace and knowledge of Jesus. Peter put the responsibility on us for growing

in God's favor and not being pulled away by false doctrine. In other passages, Paul did the same:

> Watch your life and doctrine closely. Persevere in them, because if you do, you will save both yourself and your hearers.
>
> 1 Timothy 4:16 NIV

> Therefore, my dear friends, as you have always obeyed--not only in my presence, but now much more in my absence--continue to work out your salvation with fear and trembling
>
> Philippians 2:12 NIV

If we are not serious about knowing the scriptures and living by God's principles, we could end up living by the principles of the world. Even in the religious world, we will encounter distortions of the scriptures. Some distortions may be only slightly different from the Bible, while others are directly opposed to the scriptures. We are responsible for seeking the truth, and then living and applying it to our lives.

Now let's go back to 2 Timothy 2:1 and examine the context of Paul's statement to Timothy about being strong in the grace. Paul began by wishing Timothy grace, mercy, and peace from God. This looks like a kind of shorthand for a greeting like this: "May God continue to favor you and show you mercy so you will know the peace only God can provide." To someone acquainted with the events in Paul's life and his close relationship with God, a wish for God's grace, mercy and peace was a meaningful greeting. Paul wanted the same for Timothy.

Then Paul described the foundations of his own relationship with God. He encouraged Timothy to be faithful when life was challenging (verse 5), and to never forget that God gave him a spirit of power, love and discipline (verse 7). He warned Timothy that he would suffer for the Gospel (verse 8), but that God had a purpose in mind. But the main thing was to remember that he has God's favor (verse 9)—Jesus is proof of that (verse 10).

Paul trusted God completely, and pointed to his own life as evidence of the power of God's grace (verses 11-12). He urged Timothy to faithfully follow his pattern of sound teaching out of a love for Jesus and with the help of the Holy Spirit (verses 13-14). Paul then told Timothy how everybody but one person had deserted him (verses 15-18). This brings us to Chapter 2:

> You therefore, my son, <u>be strong in the grace that is in Christ Jesus.</u> The things which you have heard from me in the presence of many witnesses, entrust these to faithful men who will be able to teach others also. Suffer hardship with me, as a good soldier of Christ Jesus. No soldier in active service entangles himself in the affairs of everyday life, so that he may please the one who enlisted him as a soldier. Also if anyone competes as an athlete, he does not win the prize unless he competes according to the rules. The hard-working farmer ought to be the first to receive his share of the crops. Consider what I say, for the Lord will give you understanding in everything. [Emphasis added.]
>
> 2 Timothy 2:1-7 NASB

This passages begins with "You therefore..." In other words, since you will face the challenges Paul described, be strong in God's favor. Here again, Paul put the responsibility for being strong squarely on Timothy shoulders—"You therefore, my son, be strong..." Don't wait for God to make it easier so you can get by without being strong.

To build anything useful, it helps to be able to visualize what the end-product should look like. Paul gave Timothy a picture of what being "strong in the grace" would look like in his life, and gave him guidance on what effort it would take. He should not think of suffering as defeat. But like a good soldier he should stay focused on the mission. He must not get distracted by the world around him. Trying to have even some of the favor of the world could keep him from giving his whole heart to God. Timothy would also need to be like a champion athlete who puts his heart into the competition and follows the rules, so as not to be disqualified. For Timothy, this meant holding on to proven spiritual principles. Timothy's mission is God's mission and God is his commanding officer. He must entrust what he learns to other faithful men, much like what Paul did for Timothy. It would not be easy, but like the hard-working farmer, Timothy would share in the reward.

Every principle that we have looked at in the previous chapters will help us be strong in God's grace. For example, if we have asked God to take away our weaknesses and that has not happened, it helps to know that God's grace is sufficient. And when we are tempted to give in to sin or worldly desires, God will give us a way out. God's grace teaches us to say "no." And in difficult times, when everything in us wants to pull back, we can instead draw near with confidence to the throne of God's grace and receive the favor and compassion we need.

Consider again the example of my sons. If they had reduced their relationship with me to just keeping my rules so that they could keep driving their car, they would have missed the biggest benefit—our relationship. The car was a short-term benefit of my favor, but they had no idea at that time how much favor they could have in the future. They did not know about all the plans I had for them as their father.

It has been a joy to watch my sons become men. They have my favor and I have theirs. And they show their favor to each other. We enjoy a loving and rewarding relationship. Likewise, God has much more in store for all of us. Be strong in the favor of God.

> "For I know the plans I have for you," declares the Lord, "plans to prosper you and not to harm you, plans to give you hope and a future. Then you will call upon me and come and pray to me, and I will listen to you. You will seek me and find me when you seek me with all your heart."
>
> Jeremiah 29:11-13 NIV

WORKSHEET 11 – Be Strong in the Grace

1. What does it mean to be strong in the grace?

_____

_____

_____

_____

_____

_____

2. What are some things we might rely on for strength rather than God?

_____

_____

_____

_____

_____

3. How would relying more on God's favor change your life?

_____

_____

_____

_____

_____

_____

4. How can we grow in God's favor?

_____

_____

_____

_____

_____

_____

_____

_____

_____

5. How does being strong in God's grace help us withstand Satan's attacks?

_____

_____

_____

_____

_____

_____

_____

_____

_____

_____

_____

Chapter Notes:

Chapter 12

Administering God's Grace

> Above all, keep fervent in your love for one another, because love covers a multitude of sins. Be hospitable to one another without complaint. As each one has received a special gift [*charisma*], employ it in serving one another as good stewards [*oikonomos*] of the manifold grace [*charis*] of God.
>
> 1 Peter 4:8-10 NASB

Until now, we have concentrated on the value of God's grace to us as individuals, and the conditions under which we receive it. In this chapter we will focus on how God's grace overflows into our relationships with each other. The NIV describes it as "faithfully administering God's grace in its various forms."

In the NASB, the word translated "stewards" is *oikonomos*. It is from *oikos* (a house or household) and *nemo* (to manage).[144] A steward manages another person's property or affairs.[145] In this case, we are called to be faithful stewards of the many forms of God's grace, and to use them to serve others. The gifts Peter is referring to are given to us because of God's favor, and are given more for the benefit of others than for ourselves.

---

144. <u>BDAG</u>, p.698.
145. <u>Webster's</u>, p. 1406.

What gift has God given you that you can use to serve others? It could be something obvious, or you may need to think about it awhile. Sometimes we do not realize we have a particular gift until God puts us in a situation where we are forced to find out what it is. Sometimes God chooses to use people who do not have an obvious gift or whose gift might seem insignificant. For example, God's favor brought out things in Gideon that were likely a surprise to everyone, including Gideon. Similarly, when Samuel invited Jesse and his sons to a sacrifice in Bethlehem (not knowing it was to learn who would be the next king over Israel), Jesse's youngest son, David, was initially left behind. But Samuel surprised everyone when the shepherd David became the guest of honor.[146] Eventually, David became a great king.

There are other good examples. The Samaritan administered God's grace when he came to the aid of a wounded stranger by giving him medical help and financial support. Dorcus sewed clothing to help the poor, and Aquila and Priscilla were known for their hospitality. Their gifts meant a great deal to the recipients.

Notice that Peter does not say, "If you happen to have a gift, you must use it." Every one of us has something to offer that God has given for the purpose of serving others. Likely, there are multiple ways we can use our gifts to be good stewards of God's grace. Even in the most challenging times of life, when we might think we are the ones who are needy, we can still pass along God's favor to others.

You may find yourself serving in a way that you never imagined. It may involve sacrifice or test your faith, or it may test the sincerity of your love by requiring you to serve people you would rather not serve. But even if using your gift makes you uncomfortable, God wants you to use it to administer His grace to others.

Administering God's grace is rewarding. It can give you so much joy that you desire to keep serving in any way you can. You may even get to serve in a way that lets you use a special talent you have, one that you really enjoy. It is interesting to note, however, how many scriptures there are that urge us to push past obstacles so that we can love and

---

146.   1 Samuel 16:1-13

serve one another. Being a good steward of God's grace is not easy. We may get into a situation where it turns out to be more difficult than we first thought it would be. Lots of things can happen that test our ability or our willingness to serve. Peter acknowledged these concerns when he described how and why we should serve others. For example, "Keep fervent in your love." We need that reminder because our love can grow cold,[147] and things can happen that test our love. The people we have the opportunity to serve may be difficult to love. Or we may feel that people have taken advantage of us in the past. But if we remember that it is God's grace that we are passing on, it will help us not take it personally when people do not respond in the way we think they should.

We are also told to "offer hospitality to one another without grumbling." Hospitality in this context does not refer to entertaining friends. The early church depended on the hospitality of members to have places to meet and to provide basic necessities for traveling missionaries.[148] Those were significant needs; needs that took sacrifice to meet. Our nature being what it is, however, the potential for grumbling or complaining is real. If we are honest, we must admit to ourselves that sometimes we want to love and serve other people, and sometimes we simply do not. We may think we have already done our fair share, or that serving in a particular way is too much to ask. Maybe our past efforts were not appreciated, so we would rather not serve. That's why Peter writes, "Keep fervent in your love for one another."

Jesus gave his disciples several opportunities to grow in their love and willingness to serve other people. Here is one of the most memorable:

> When Jesus landed and saw a large crowd, he had compassion on them, because they were like sheep without a shepherd. So he began teaching them many things.
>
> By this time it was late in the day, so his disciples came to him. "This is a remote place," they said, "and it's already very late. Send the people away so they can go to the surrounding

---

147. Matthew 24:12 NIV

148. Barclay on 1 Peter 4:9.

countryside and villages and buy themselves something to eat."

But he answered, "You give them something to eat."

They said to him, "That would take eight months of a man's wages! Are we to go and spend that much on bread and give it to them to eat?"

Mark 6:34-37 NIV

Jesus used this occasion and others like it to help his disciples learn as they served people to rely more on God. That is something we also must learn. In the verse that follows our theme passage for this chapter, Peter explained how God must be our source of direction and strength when we serve:

If anyone speaks, he should do it as one <u>speaking the very words of God</u>. If anyone serves, he should do it <u>with the strength God provides,</u> so that in all things God may be praised through Jesus Christ. To him be the glory and the power for ever and ever. Amen. [Emphasis added.]

1 Peter 4:11 NIV

This instruction applies to all of us. Our words should bring praise and glory to God. Something as simple as a few gracious words can be a demonstration of God's grace. Think about the nature of the many words you hear on a typical day. How many would you say were gracious? Even in Jesus' day, gracious words stood out:

All spoke well of him and were amazed at the gracious [*charis*] words that came from his lips. "Isn't this Joseph's son?" they asked.

Luke 4:22 NIV

Gracious speech has even more impact when words of a different sort might be expected.

Let your conversation be always full of grace [*charis*], seasoned with salt, so that you may know how to answer everyone.

Colossians 4:6 NIV

> Let no unwholesome word proceed from your mouth, but only such a word as is good for edification according to the need of the moment, so that it will give grace [*charis*] to those who hear.
>
> Ephesians 4:29 NASB

Angry, accusing or unloving words tear down. Gracious words are encouraging, comforting, and reassuring—they build up and strengthen relationships. The Bible gives us great direction about our speech.

It is difficult to administer God's grace if we rely on our own strength. Peter said, "If anyone serves, he should do it with the strength God provides." Showing God's favor to others takes physical and emotional energy—sometimes more than we think we have, and that's when we get to serve with the strength God provides.

Paul wrote that God gives us gifts for the benefit of others, not because we are so special. He also warned us to not become prideful if we receive recognition or praise for our gifts:

> But to each one of us grace [*charis*] has been given as Christ apportioned it.
>
> Ephesians 4:7 NIV

> For by the grace [*charis*] given me I say to every one of you: Do not think of yourself more highly than you ought, but rather think of yourself with sober judgment, in accordance with the measure of faith God has given you. Just as each of us has one body with many members, and these members do not all have the same function, so in Christ we who are many form one body, and each member belongs to all the others. [Emphasis added.]
>
> Romans 12:3-5 NIV

Paul received a measure of faith that allowed him to do incredible things, but he was just one part of the body. Other needs in the body were met by gifts God gave to others. There are many ways we can serve:

> We have different gifts [*charisma*], according to the grace
> [*charis*] given us. If a man's gift is prophesying, let him use
> it in proportion to his faith. If it is serving, let him serve; if it
> is teaching, let him teach; if it is encouraging, let him encour-
> age; if it is contributing to the needs of others, let him give
> generously; if it is leadership, let him govern diligently; if it
> is showing mercy, let him do it cheerfully.
>
> Romans 12:6-8 NIV

There are more gifts than are listed in this passage. The point is more about how we get gifts and how we can use them than about what our gift might be or its importance. God intended for us to use our gifts diligently, faithfully, cheerfully and liberally.

To some degree, we are *all* commanded to do some of the things Paul described as gifts. For example, we all must be merciful (if we do not show mercy, we will not receive mercy). However, there are people who are more gifted at showing mercy than others. You might think that you would not want this particular gift, but we do not get to choose the gifts God gives us. We are to faithfully administer God's grace in whatever way he enables us.

What gift(s) do you have? Do you have the gift of encouragement? Are you able to help others face difficult trials because you were faith-ful through a similar trial? Is your gift teaching and inspiring others with the Word? Are you able to give liberally to support the work of the church? Paul urged the Corinthian church to "excel in this grace [*charis*] of giving."[149]

When we administer God's grace, we are passing on to others what He has given to us. How we think about His favor influences how will-ing we are to share. An exchange between my wife and one of my sons is a simple illustration. My wife bought my five-year-old son a package of gum. When his younger brother asked him to share, his immediate response was, "No, its mine." She reminded him that just ten minutes

---

149. 2 Corinthians 8:7 NIV

earlier, he did not have any gum either, and he only had it now because she gave it to him. He thought about it a minute then decided to share with his brother. In a similar way, we can be possessive about a gift God has given us and act like it is soley for our own enjoyment. But God has given us special gifts for the purpose of serving others:

> Each one should use whatever gift he has received to serve others, faithfully administering God's grace in its various forms.
>
> 1 Peter 4:10 NIV

We do not need to worry about having enough of God's grace. God never gets tired of showing it! And God's grace never wears out. By God's grace, we have received many blessings, and we are blessed to be able to administer God's grace to others.

WORKSHEET 12 – Administering God's Grace

1. Why does God rely on us to administer his grace to each other?

_____

_____

_____

_____

2. What gifts do you have? How can you use them to administer God's grace to other people?

_____

_____

_____

_____

_____

_____

_____

3. What obstacles must we overcome to administer God's favor to others?

_____

_____

_____

_____

_____

_____

_____

Chapter Notes:

Chapter 13

The Effect of Grace

> For I am the least of the apostles and do not even deserve
> to be called an apostle, because I persecuted the church of
> God. But by the grace [*charis*] of God I am what I am, and
> his grace [*charis*] to me was not without effect. No, I worked
> harder than all of them--yet not I, but the grace [*charis*] of
> God that was with me.
>
> 1 Corinthians 15:9-10 NIV

The Apostle Paul wrote more about God's grace than any other Biblical
writer. Here he credits the grace (favor) of God for the amazing turn-
around in his life. Paul went from zealously persecuting anyone pro-
fessing to know Jesus to preaching Him powerfully. Paul's source of
strength and inspiration to work hard was the favor he felt from God.

Paul's life was a demonstration of the impact of the favor of God.
However, not everyone who experiences God's favor is transformed.
Here are some reasons why grace could be "without effect" in our
lives:

- We act like we do not need it.

- We admit that we need it, but do nothing about it.

- We think we have God's grace because we deserve it.

- We care more about pleasing ourselves than about pleasing God.

- We value the world's favor more than God's favor.

- We go about life unaware of how God is working.

- When we suffer, we think God must be against us.

In one way or another, Satan has a hand in everything that prevents us from enjoying the favor of God. He has used schemes and lies to deceive man since the beginning. He will do what he can to discredit God and keep us from having a close relationship with Him, so we will miss out on the power of His favor in our lives. Satan also wins if we become distracted by the cares of this world and fail to see how God is working. But with God's favor, we can overcome Satan's schemes. We can say no to sin and worldly passions, and live self-controlled and godly lives. When we are tempted, we can take the way of escape that God has given us. And God's favor changes our perspective of trials and helps us faithfully face things that are out of our control.

Think about the daily battle to be close to God. Understanding that God's grace affects what happens in our lives *today*—not just eternally—will have a great impact on our relationship with Him. This is important to understand. Limiting our view of God's grace to our future salvation can cause us to overlook how His grace affects what will happen today. If we are not looking for the impact of God's grace, we probably will not see it. That is one reason why it is so helpful to think of God's grace as his favor. Then if we look for how God is favoring us, we can see his favor at work in our lives every day. That will remind us that God is near us and wants to be very involved in our lives. Then having God's favor today will matter to us, and our relationship with God will feel more personal.

Have you felt the favor of God? How has it impacted your life? There are so many possibilities. One way that God's favor should impact all of us is that we should be thankful and express our gratitude to God. Thankfulness is an important aspect of our relationship with God. Consider the following verses where *charis* is translated as "thank" or "thanks":

> I thank [*charis*] Christ Jesus our Lord, who has given me strength, that he considered me faithful, appointing me to his service.
>
> 1 Timothy 1:12 NIV

> But thanks [*charis*] be to God! He gives us the victory through our Lord Jesus Christ.
>
> 1 Corinthians 15:57 NIV

> Thanks [*charis*] be to God for his indescribable gift!
>
> 2 Corinthians 9:15 NIV

Remember that the simple description of *charis* is to show favor. In these verses, Paul expressed his *charis* to Jesus and God. Have you ever thought you could show grace to God? This is the reason praying before a meal is sometimes referred to as "saying grace." Saying grace is a simple but important way of offering our favor to God. It is a privilege to be able to speak to God and express our favor by thanking Him for all he has done for us.

The idea that we can show grace to God may seem like a bit of a stretch, given how badly we need His grace. But remember that we have a personal relationship with God. He is our Heavenly Father and we are His adopted children.[150] And even a child can show favor to his father. Picture a father playing with his young son. The son's expressions of joy and affection let the father know that his son is delighted by his love and attention. It warms the father's heart. If you are a parent, you know what I mean.

Not only can we show our appreciation to God through our words, we can also give thanks by what we do with our lives:

---

150. Galatians 4:1-6; Romans 8:15-23

> And whatever you do, whether in word or deed, do it all in the name of the Lord Jesus, giving thanks [*eucharisteo*] to God the Father through him.
>
> Colossians 3:17 NIV

In this verse, the Greek word translated as "thanks" is *eucharisteo*. The root words of *eucharisteo* are *eu*, which means well or good; and *charizomai* which means to show favor, give freely.[151] When we do things in the name of Jesus and give him the credit for our lives, we are showing our favor to God.

We can also express our favor to God through songs of praise. We do not have to have a great voice; what matters more is what we feel in our hearts:

> Let the word of Christ dwell in you richly as you teach and admonish one another with all wisdom, and as you sing psalms, hymns and spiritual songs with gratitude [*charis*] in your hearts to God.
>
> Colossians 3:16 NIV

Gratitude is essential to build a stronger relationship with God. If we are not grateful, we need to carefully examine our hearts. Not being thankful to God is an indication that His grace is without effect in our lives. To illustrate the importance of thankfulness, consider Luke's account of Jesus' encounter with ten men who had leprosy. Note the responses of the lepers to the favor shown them by Jesus:

> As he was going into a village, ten men who had leprosy met him. They stood at a distance and called out in a loud voice, "Jesus, Master, have pity on us!" When he saw them, he said, "Go, show yourselves to the priests." And as they went, they were cleansed. One of them, when he saw he was healed, came back, praising God in a loud voice. He threw himself at Jesus' feet and thanked [*eucharisteo*] him--and he was a Samaritan. Jesus asked, "Were not all ten cleansed?

---

151.   James Strong, <u>Strong's Talking Greek & Hebrew Dictionary</u>, WORD*search* 8.0.2.40 (WORD*search* Corp, 2008).

Where are the other nine? Was no one found to return and give praise to God except this foreigner?"

Luke 17:12-18 NIV

Jesus was astonished that nine of the men did not thank him for essentially giving them back their lives. For that amazing gift, only one man took the time to praise God. What were the others thinking? Were they just too busy enjoying the blessing they received to show their gratitude? God's grace apparently had no effect on their hearts. It seems they cared about God's favor when they were desperate, but not after they were healed. We can only guess that when their future began to look bright, they thought they could handle things on their own from that point forward. They went off to enjoy their new lives and forgot about Jesus.

An obvious lesson from the story is that we should never take God's favor for granted. A less obvious lesson is that if we are not grateful for what God has already done to show us His favor, it is doubtful that receiving more favor would ever make us feel more grateful. The nine showed that even a great blessing can be minimized or taken for granted. Not only did they miss an opportunity to show their gratitude to Jesus, they missed the opportunity of their lives to pursue an ongoing relationship with Him. Sadly, they just went on their way.

There are many great biblical examples of the life-changing effects of God's favor. Reading about Abraham, Moses, Peter and many others can open our eyes to the power and possibilities of God's favor in our own lives. It can bring changes we would not expect or cannot even imagine. Remember that some who received God's favor were not initially seeking God or even aware that God was at work in their lives. For example, evil King Manasseh sought God only after his captors put a hook in his nose. But when he humbled himself, God showed him incredible favor by reinstating him as King. Then Manasseh led the people back to worshipping God. Gideon, another good example, went from hiding out in a wine press to defeating a powerful army when he finally let himself be convinced that he had the favor of God.

Finding God's favor in our lives is an adventure we do not want to miss. What a disappointment it would be to miss out on a daily loving relationship with God. This is what happened to the older brother in the story of the prodigal son. He obeyed and worked hard for his father everyday, but more out of duty than because of their relationship. In the end, he felt he had nothing to celebrate. Rather than feeling like a favored son, he felt like a servant.

God is our father, and he wants us to be his sons and daughters:

> As God has said: "I will live with them and walk among them, and I will be their God, and they will be my people. Therefore come out from them and be separate, says the Lord. Touch no unclean thing, and I will receive you. I will be a Father to you, and you will be my sons and daughters, says the Lord Almighty."
>
> 2 Corinthians 6:16b-18 NIV

God wants to live with us, walk with us and receive us. He has done everything necessary to open the door for us, and now it depends on us. The choice is ours. We can choose to seek the favor of the world or the favor of God. We cannot have both. The favor of the world comes in attractive packages and offers short-term rewards. But do not be fooled; the world cannot deliver on its promises. However, God will keep His promises, and His promises are unmatched by anything in the world. God can and will reward us for putting our faith in His favor.[152] God gives us "greater grace."[153] Consider these encouraging scriptures about God:

> The Lord is gracious and righteous; our God is full of compassion. The Lord protects the simplehearted; when I was in great need, he saved me. Be at rest once more, O my soul, for the Lord has been good to you.
>
> Psalm 116:5-7 NIV

---

152.   Hebrews 11:6

153.   James 4:6 NASB

Yet the Lord longs to be gracious to you; he rises to show you compassion. For the Lord is a God of justice. Blessed are all who wait for him!

Isaiah 30:18 NIV

The Lord loves righteousness and justice; the earth is full of his unfailing love.

Psalm 33:5 NIV

Rend your heart and not your garments. Return to the Lord your God, for he is gracious and compassionate, slow to anger and abounding in love, and he relents from sending calamity.

Joel 2:13 NIV

Your kingdom is an everlasting kingdom, and your dominion endures through all generations. The Lord is faithful to all his promises and loving toward all he has made.

Psalm 145:13 NIV

However, as it is written: "No eye has seen, no ear has heard, no mind has conceived what God has prepared for those who love him."

1 Corinthians 2:9 NIV

For I know the plans I have for you," declares the Lord, "plans to prosper you and not to harm you, plans to give you hope and a future. Then you will call upon me and come and pray to me, and I will listen to you. You will seek me and find me when you seek me with all your heart.

Jeremiah 29:11-13 NIV

Finally, I want to remind you that seeking God's favor is a lifetime journey. Like Abraham, who gave us a tremendous example of faith and obedience, we must be patient as we look to God for His favor. He knows what is best for us and loves us deeply. He wants nothing more than to help us get to heaven. He is showing favor even when He says no to our requests or does not give us what we think we need when we think we need it. Hold on tightly to the truth about grace found in God's word:[154]

- Grace and peace be yours in abundance.

- It is good for our hearts to be strengthened by grace.

- Do not receive God's grace in vain.

- Approach the throne of grace with confidence.

- Continue in the grace of God.

- Grow in the grace.

- Be strong in the grace.

- Set your hope fully on the grace to be given you when Jesus is revealed.

- See to it that no one misses the grace of God.

---

154. 1 Peter 1:2; Hebrews 13:9; 2 Corinthians 6:1; Hebrews 4:16; Acts 13:43; 2 Peter 3:18; 2 Timothy 2:1; 1 Peter 1:13; and Hebrews 12:15

WORKSHEET 13 – The Effect of Grace

1. How does God's favor inspire people to work hard?

---

2. How does knowing you have the favor of God change how you handle the cares of the world?

---

3. Think about your week. What did you say no to because you felt the favor of God?

---

4. How has growing in your understanding of God's grace empowered you to face things that seemed too difficult before?

_____

_____

_____

_____

_____

_____

_____

_____

_____

_____

5. How has God's grace changed your life?

_____

_____

_____

_____

_____

_____

_____

_____

_____

_____

_____

_____

_____

Chapter Notes:

Silverday Press Books:

A Gentle &
Quiet Spirit
- Revised Edition -

Discover the Truth About
These Misunderstood Qualities

By Virginia Lefler

A NEW PERSPECTIVE FOR TODAY'S CHRISTIAN WOMAN

...the unfading beauty of a gentle and quiet spirit, which is
of great worth in God's sight.
- 1 Peter 3:4

Many Christian women face a dilemma in embracing the biblical teaching about a gentle and quiet spirit. They want to please God but they perceive "gentle" and "quiet" as weak or passive qualities. The truth is that the original Greek text describes a strong and peaceful woman, and the word translated as "great worth" means the very end or limit with reference to value. In other words, there is nothing more valuable to God. This book will give you a new perspective and some valuable lessons in how to become this strong woman with inner peace. Twenty-five worksheets throughout the book make it especially useful as a personal or group study guide.

BOOKS AND FREE TEACHING AIDS ARE AVAILABLE AT:

www.SilverdayPress.com

Pursuing Purity

Protection, Power and Peace
for Every Christian Woman

By Virginia Lefler

In a world of declining standards, purity is seldom honored or pursued. In fact, many women believe that a worldly woman is strong and secure while a woman who strives for purity and strength from God is naïve and vulnerable. Nothing could be further from the truth. A worldly woman is more hardened than strong and her security depends mostly on the day's events. To find real strength and be secure in our world, we must know and embrace God's timeless standards for purity.

Pursuing Purity offers hope and solutions. Discover the protection, power and peace that God promises to those who purify themselves. Worksheets throughout the book make it especially useful as a personal or group study guide.

BOOKS AND FREE TEACHING AIDS ARE AVAILABLE AT:

www.SilverdayPress.com